how to
fill in your
2004
tax return
the easy way

GRAHAM M KITCHEN FCA

Consultant Editors
Chris Maddock and Karen Foster ATT
of BDO Stoy Hayward,
Chartered Accountants

foulsham
LONDON • NEW YORK • TORONTO • SYDNEY

foulsham

The Publishing House, Bennetts Close
Cippenham, Slough, Berkshire SL1 5AP

ISBN 0-572-02961-6

Printed in Great Britain by St. Edmundsbury Press, Bury St. Edmunds, Suffolk

Contents

Introduction

How to use this book

When you get any tax form, identify it in the contents page of this book, turn to the appropriate chapter and you can see what you need to do with the form. If the form needs to be filled in, this book will tell you how to do this, where to get the information – plus a few tax tips along the way! There is a summary of rates and allowances, including those announced in the March 2004 Budget, on page 97.

Tax return form

Not everyone gets a tax return automatically. They are normally sent out to people who have more than one source of income or are higher-rate taxpayers; to all company directors; to the self-employed and to anyone whose tax affairs are fairly complex.

The fact that you do not get a tax return doesn't mean that you don't have to complete one.

The responsibility is yours – not your employer's, nor the tax office's. If you have received earnings or income which hasn't been taxed, or you think you have paid too much tax and you are entitled to a tax refund, then you should fill in a tax return.

You have the opportunity to work out, on tax calculation forms, your own tax liability or tax refund if you so wish (see pages 91–92).

You can submit your tax return electronically via the internet on www.ir-efile.gov.uk/ – see pages 89–90 on some hints as to how to do this efficiently.

Where do you get a form?

If you want a tax return form, contact your local tax office; if you want the supplementary pages, telephone the special Inland Revenue order line on 0845 9000 404. You will need to quote your name, address and NI reference number. You can also request forms and notes in large print, audio or in Braille format by contacting your local tax office. The Inland Revenue have a helpline which you can ring on 0845 9000 444. There is also a website – www.inlandrevenue.gov.uk/sa – from which you can download forms, or you can order by e-mail on saorderline.ir@gtnet.gov.uk

When should you fill in a tax return?

Unfortunately, the tax year does not follow the calendar year – it runs from 6 April to 5 April – just to confuse everyone!

The 2004 tax return covers your income, capital gains, reliefs and allowances for the year ended 5 April 2004.

Although it is called a self assessment tax return, you do not have to calculate your own tax if you don't want to. Provided that you send in your tax return by 30 September 2004 (or two months after the date the tax return was sent to you, if later), the tax office will do it for you. If you file your tax return on-line then your tax will be calculated automatically.

If you wish to use the tax calculator working sheets provided with your tax return, then you have until 31 January 2005 to send in your return (see page 88).

Payments on account

If you have not paid most of your tax by deduction, or you are self-employed, you should have paid an amount on account of your 2003–2004 tax liability on 31 January 2004 (see page 38).

Don't be late

There will be an automatic penalty of £100 if your tax return is not sent in by 31 January 2005 and another £100 six months later if it is still overdue. (These are reduced if the tax due is less than £200.)

In addition, a surcharge will be levied of 5 per cent of any tax due by 31 January if

unpaid at 28 February, and a further 5 per cent if unpaid by 31 July (plus interest on the first surcharge).

There are further penalties if you are persistently late – as much as £60 a day!

There are also fines of up to £3,000 for each failure to keep adequate records to support figures in your tax return. You have been warned!

Do you have to fill in a tax return if you are always due a refund?

No; the tax office will probably send you a form R40, which is a simplified form of return and which should result in your tax refund coming through regularly and quickly (see page 78).

Go back six years

If you find you have been paying too much tax this year, there is a good chance that this has happened in previous years. You can go back six years to reclaim tax.

Are you claiming tax refunds due to you?

The Inland Revenue estimates that around seven million pensioners, married women and children are not claiming their tax refunds.

If your total income does not exceed your tax allowances and you have received any income from which tax has been deducted, you should claim it back. Turn to page 78 for advice on what to do or telephone the taxback helpline on 0845 077 6543.

If you are on PAYE

Don't assume that your PAYE code is correct. Your employer cannot check it for you – you must do it yourself (see page 76); it's also up to you to check that the tax that you have paid during the year is correct (see page 77).

What to do if you don't get a reply from your tax office

Under the Taxpayer's Charter you should not have to wait more than eight weeks for a reply to your query. Contact your local tax enquiry office if you have a query, then your tax inspector.

If you still do not get satisfaction, write to the director of your regional tax office and as a last resort to the Adjudicator's Office at 28 Haymarket, London SW1Y 4SP – all telephone numbers are in the telephone directory under Inland Revenue. You will find more information in Inland Revenue leaflet IR120.

How this book can help you

1 Each page corresponds to a section of your tax return or tax form, and you are told what to enter, what *not* to enter and where to find the information that the tax office needs.
2 There are many tax tips and additional chapters to give you extra advice in claiming tax back and checking your own tax.
3 It will tell you whether you are due a tax refund and, more importantly, how to claim it.
4 You will avoid paying too much tax because you can identify the form you have received and know what to do with it.
5 You can fill in the tax return form reproduced in this book so that you have a permanent copy to which you can refer at any time.
6 It will give you a better understanding as to how the tax system works so you can use it to your best advantage.

How to fill in your tax return

Start filling in your 2004 self-assessment tax return by reading questions Q1 to Q9 and ticking any 'Yes' box on page 2 of the return (reproduced below) that applies to you.

If you tick 'Yes' in any box, check to see if the tax office have sent you the supplementary pages to complete and tick them off in the right-hand column.

You will need supplementary pages if you are:

	Ref No.	Page in this book
Employed	SA101	39
Participating in share schemes	SA102	46
Self-employed	SA103	50
In partnership	SA104	57
Owning land or property	SA105	59
Receiving foreign income	SA106	63
Receiving income from trusts or estates	SA107	68
Declaring capital gains or losses	SA108	70
Non-resident in the UK	SA109	75

If you need supplementary pages and you have not been sent them with your tax return, ring the Inland Revenue order line on 0845 9000 404 (fax 0845 9000 604) and ask for the missing pages. These forms can also be downloaded from their website at inlandrevenue.gov.uk/sa. You will need to quote your name, address and National Insurance reference number.

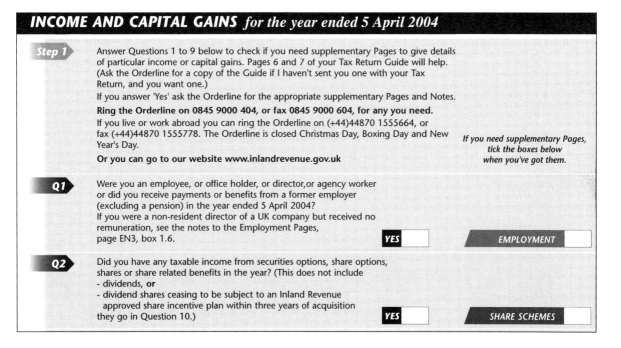

INCOME AND CAPITAL GAINS *for the year ended 5 April 2004*

Step 1 Answer Questions 1 to 9 below to check if you need supplementary Pages to give details of particular income or capital gains. Pages 6 and 7 of your Tax Return Guide will help. (Ask the Orderline for a copy of the Guide if I haven't sent you one with your Tax Return, and you want one.)
If you answer 'Yes' ask the Orderline for the appropriate supplementary Pages and Notes.
Ring the Orderline on 0845 9000 404, or fax 0845 9000 604, for any you need.
If you live or work abroad you can ring the Orderline on (+44)44870 1555664, or fax (+44)44870 1555778. The Orderline is closed Christmas Day, Boxing Day and New Year's Day.
Or you can go to our website www.inlandrevenue.gov.uk

If you need supplementary Pages, tick the boxes below when you've got them.

Q1 Were you an employee, or office holder, or director,or agency worker or did you receive payments or benefits from a former employer (excluding a pension) in the year ended 5 April 2004?
If you were a non-resident director of a UK company but received no remuneration, see the notes to the Employment Pages, page EN3, box 1.6.
YES | EMPLOYMENT

Q2 Did you have any taxable income from securities options, share options, shares or share related benefits in the year? (This does not include
- dividends, **or**
- dividend shares ceasing to be subject to an Inland Revenue approved share incentive plan within three years of acquisition they go in Question 10.)
YES | SHARE SCHEMES

Q3	Were you self-employed (but not in partnership)? (You should also tick 'Yes' if you were a Name at Lloyd's.)	YES ☐	SELF-EMPLOYMENT ☐
Q4	Were you in partnership?	YES ☐	PARTNERSHIP ☐
Q5	Did you receive any rent or other income from land and property in the UK?	YES ☐	LAND & PROPERTY ☐

Q6	Did you have any taxable income from overseas pensions or benefits, or from foreign companies or savings institutions, offshore funds or trusts abroad, or from land and property abroad or gains on foreign insurance policies?	YES ☐	
	Have you or could you have received, or enjoyed directly or indirectly, or benefited in any way from, income of a foreign entity as a result of a transfer of assets made in this or earlier years?	YES ☐	
	Do you want to claim foreign tax credit relief for foreign tax paid on foreign income or gains?	YES ☐	FOREIGN ☐

Q7	Did you receive, or are you deemed to have, income from a trust, settlement or the residue of a deceased person's estate?	YES ☐	TRUSTS ETC ☐

Q8	Capital gains - read the guidance on page 7 of the Tax Return Guide.		
	• If you have disposed of your only or main residence do you need the Capital Gains Pages?	YES ☐	
	• Did you dispose of other chargeable assets worth more than £31,600 in total?	YES ☐	
	• Answer 'Yes' if:		
	– allowable losses are deducted from your chargeable gains, which total more than £7,900 before deduction and before taper relief, or		
	– no allowable losses are deducted from your chargeable gains and after taper relief your taxable gains total more than £7,900 or		
	– you want to make a claim or election for the year.	YES ☐	CAPITAL GAINS ☐

Q9	Are you claiming that you were not resident, or not ordinarily resident, or not domiciled, in the UK, or dual resident in the UK and another country, for all or part of the year?	YES ☐	NON-RESIDENCE ETC ☐

Step 2 Fill in any supplementary Pages BEFORE going to Step 3.

Please use blue or black ink to fill in your Tax Return and please do not include pence. Round down your income and gains. Round up your tax credits and tax deductions. Round to the nearest pound.

When you have filled in all the supplementary Pages you need, tick this box. ☐

Step 3 Fill in Questions 10 to 24. If you answer 'Yes', fill in the relevant boxes. If not applicable, go to the next question.

The next step

If you have ticked any of the 'Yes' boxes above, then the next step is to fill in those supplementary pages – turn to the appropriate page reference in this book before you go on to complete the rest of the tax return.

If you have not ticked any 'Yes' boxes, then start to fill in page 3 of your tax return, which covers income from UK savings and investments.

The tax return is reproduced on the following pages.

There is a 'Fill this in if ...' prompt after each question so that you can identify quickly whether it applies to you or not. If it does, there are prompts telling you where to find the information and what to enter.

There are lots of tax tips and reminders along the way.

All of the boxes throughout the whole of the tax return and supplementary pages are numbered – so just follow the numbers.

Q10 Income from UK savings and investments

If you receive income from savings with UK banks, building societies or deposit takers, or receive untaxed income from a bare trust as a beneficiary or any taxable cash payment following a building society merger or conversion, tick the 'Yes' box and fill in the information requested.

If this section does not apply to you, then turn to Q11 on page 13.

Q10 Did you receive any income from UK savings and investments? **YES**

If yes, tick this box and then fill in boxes 10.1 to 10.26 as appropriate. Include only your share from any joint savings and investments. If not applicable, go to Question 11.

Bank and building society interest 10.1 – 10.4

Fill this in if
You have savings with banks, building societies and deposit takers in the UK, including UK internet accounts.

Where to find the information
Your bank, building society, etc. should send you an annual statement showing the interest earned and any tax deducted.

You will need to keep a note of how you arrive at the totals – use the tax organiser on page 100 of this book.

■ *Interest*

● Interest from UK banks or building societies. (Interest from UK Internet accounts should be included) *If you have more than one bank or building society account enter **totals** in the boxes.*

- enter any bank or building society interest that **has not had tax taken off**. (Most of this interest is taxed before you receive it so make sure you should be filling in box 10.1, rather than boxes 10.2 to 10.4.) Enter other types of interest in boxes 10.5 to 10.14 as appropriate.

Taxable amount
10.1 £

- enter details of your **taxed** bank or building society interest. *The Working Sheet on page 10 of your Tax Return Guide will help you fill in boxes 10.2 to 10.4.*

Amount **after** tax deducted	Tax deducted	Gross amount **before** tax
10.2 £	**10.3** £	**10.4** £

What to enter
Where tax has been deducted, fill in boxes 10.2, 10.3 and 10.4 with the totals.

Where no tax has been deducted, fill in box 10.1 with the total amount you received in the year ended 5 April 2004.

Do not include
The name of the bank, building society, etc.

If you receive income from an offshore bank do not enter it here; it goes in the Foreign income boxes (see page 63).

Do not include National Savings interest.

Tax tip Interest gross or net of tax?
If your total income in 2004–2005 is likely to be less than your personal allowance (see page 97), complete and sign form R85, or your bank or building society will deduct tax from your interest rather than paying it gross and you will have to reclaim it at the end of the year (see page 78).

Tax tip Joint names
Interest on savings or investments held in joint names is divided equally. If ownership is not held equally, declare the split on tax office form 17, then enter the amounts in your tax returns. This declaration takes effect from the date it is made, if you send the form to the tax office within 60 days.

Unit trust interest 10.5 – 10.7

Fill this in if
You have interest from UK unit trusts, etc.

Where to find the information
Your unit trust, etc. will provide you with a tax voucher.

You will need to keep a note of how you arrive at the totals – use the tax organiser on page 100 of this book.

• Interest distributions from UK authorised unit trusts and open-ended investment companies (dividend distributions go below)	Amount **after** tax deducted	Tax deducted	Gross amount **before** tax
	10.5 £	**10.6** £	**10.7** £

What to enter
The total gross amount, total tax deducted and total after tax including any interest reinvested in accumulation units in shares.

If you received interest without tax being deducted, include the figure in 10.7, with a zero value in your total for box 10.6.

Do not include
Any equalisation reserves; nor any dividend distributions from unit trusts – they go in 10.18 – 10.20.

National Savings interest 10.8 – 10.11

Fill this in if
You have any interest from a National Savings ordinary account (apart from the first £70) or investment accounts, income or capital bonds, deposit bonds, Pensioners' Guaranteed Income Bonds, FIRST Option Bonds or Fixed Rate Savings Bonds.

National Savings Guaranteed equity bonds go in 10.14

Where to find the information
If you receive interest from a National Savings ordinary account, send your book to National Savings, Glasgow, G58 1SB to have the interest added. Show the total interest in your tax return but exclude the first £70 of interest as it is tax free.

Interest is credited automatically on your investment account every 31 December and a statement will be sent to you if you request one. The tax office will accept this December interest figure as the figure to go in your tax return; you do not have to apportion it on a time basis. National Savings will send you an annual statement of interest earned on bonds in April each year.

• National Savings & Investments (other than First Option Bonds and Fixed Rate Savings Bonds and the first £70 of interest from an Ordinary Account)			Taxable amount
			10.8 £

• National Savings & Investments First Option Bonds and Fixed Rate Savings Bonds	Amount **after** tax deducted	Tax deducted	Gross amount **before** tax
	10.9 £	**10.10** £	**10.11** £

What to enter
The total interest received or credited to your National Savings accounts and bonds in the year ended 5 April 2004 goes in box 10.8. Interest from Bonds will have had tax deducted so fill in the boxes 10.9, 10.10 and 10.11 for these.

Do not include
Interest from any National Savings Certificates or Children's Bonus Bonds – these do not have to be declared in your tax return. Neither do you need to give details of any Premium Bond or Lotto winnings.

All other interest 10.12 – 10.14

Fill this in if
You have any interest from UK savings, etc. not covered in the earlier sections. These could include, for example, purchased annuities (but not those arising from a personal pension or retirement contract); interest from Government stocks; friendly societies. This section could also be used for profits on relevant discounted securities and interest on certificates of tax deposits, etc.

Where to find the information
Annuity statements and other documentation, certificates and interest vouchers from investment and insurance companies.

> **Tax tip** Tax on interest
> If most of your income comes from interest you may be due a tax refund (see page 78).
>   You can request that interest from Government stocks is paid gross to save you having to claim back the tax if you are on low income.

	Amount after tax deducted	Tax deducted	Gross amount before tax
● Other income from UK savings and investments (except dividends)	**10.12** £	**10.13** £	**10.14** £

What to enter
The total amount received, tax credit or tax deducted and gross income.

   If you have accrued income reliefs exceeding charges, the net figure should be deducted from box 10.14 without any adjustment to box 10.13. If charges exceed reliefs, use box 10.14.

Do not include
Any dividends – this section is for interest only, retirement annuities and other pension schemes are covered in Q11 (page 13).

   You can disregard accrued income reliefs and charges if the nominal value of your accrued income securities was below £5,000 in the period 6 April 2002 to 5 April 2004.

Dividend income 10.15 – 10.20

Fill this in if
You received dividends or distributions from UK companies including dividends from trusts, unit trusts and oeics.

Where to find the information
The dividend vouchers and distribution receipts will show all these details.

■ *Dividends*			
	Dividend/distribution	Tax credit	Dividend/distribution plus credit
● Dividends and other qualifying distributions from UK companies	**10.15** £	**10.16** £	**10.17** £
● Dividend distributions from UK authorised unit trusts and open-ended investment companies	**10.18** £	**10.19** £	**10.20** £

What to enter
Put in each of the boxes the total amounts you received, the tax credit (or notional income tax) and the gross amount (the dividend received plus the tax credit).

Do not include
Any equalisation receipts, nor any dividends received from your own personal service company if you have claimed relief and the Inland Revenue has ruled that they are non-taxable in your hands under 'IR35' rules.

Dividend income 10.21 – 10.26

Fill this in if

You received scrip dividends (new shares instead of a cash dividend) and non-qualifying distributions and loans written off.

Where to find the information

Your dividend distribution statement will show the scrip cash equivalent (10.21), the notional tax will be 11.11% (10.22) which, when added to the 10.21 figure, will give you the figure to go in box 10.23. Similarly with the next line of boxes.

	Dividend	Notional tax	Dividend **plus** notional tax
● Scrip dividends from UK companies	**10.21** £	**10.22** £	**10.23** £

	Distribution/Loan	Notional tax	Taxable amount
● Non-qualifying distributions and loans written off	**10.24** £	**10.25** £	**10.26** £

What to enter

The amount you received in 10.24; add 11.11% as the notional tax in 10.25; add the two figures together to go in 10.26. For distributions, enter the amount received in 10.26 and multiply this by 10% and put this figure in 10.25. Leave 10.24 blank.

> **Tax tip** Tax credit
> If you pay tax at the starting or basic rate, the tax credit (10%) on dividends generally meets your tax bill on this income. If you are a higher-rate taxpayer the tax credit is treated as a payment on account of any tax due. If, however, you are a non-taxpayer you cannot reclaim this tax credit.

Q11 Income from a UK pension, retirement annuity or Social Security Benefit

If you received income from a taxable UK pension, retirement annuity or social security benefit, tick the 'Yes' box and fill in the information requested.

If not, turn to Q12 on page 16.

Q11 **Did you receive a taxable UK pension, retirement annuity, Social Security benefit or Statutory Payment?**
Read the notes on pages 13 to 15 of the Tax Return Guide.

YES

If yes, tick this box and then fill in boxes 11.1 to 11.14 as appropriate.
If not applicable, go to Question 12.

State pensions and benefits 11.1 – 11.5

Fill this in if
You were entitled to a state pension or other pension listed below, or a jobseeker's allowance between 6 April 2003 and 5 April 2004.

Where to find the information
You should have a statement from the Department for Work and Pensions (DWP) of the pensions and allowances which were paid to you – if not, ask at your local office.

■ State pensions and benefits		Taxable amount for 2003-04
● State Retirement Pension - *enter the total of your entitlements for the year*	**11.1**	£
● Widow's Pension or Bereavement Allowance	**11.2**	£
● Widowed Mother's Allowance or Widowed Parent's Allowance	**11.3**	£
● Industrial Death Benefit Pension	**11.4**	£
● Jobseeker's Allowance	**11.5**	£

What to enter
Any basic State pension including any earnings-related pension, graduated pension and age addition. A married man should only enter amounts payable to him; a married woman should enter amounts payable to her in her tax return (even if paid as a result of her husband's contributions). Include any earnings-related increase with the widowed mother's allowance but exclude any child-dependency increase.

Do not include
The State Christmas bonus or Winter Fuel payment or amount paid for a dependent child.

> **Tax tip** State pension income
> If the State pension is going to be your only income, then you can, and should, apply for pension credit by telephoning 0800 99 1234. You should also apply to your local DWP office for various other social security benefits which are not taxable and need not be included in your tax return. Also apply to your local council for housing benefit and a reduction in your council tax.

State benefits 11.6 – 11.9

Fill this in if

You received or were entitled to any of the following benefits in the year ended 5 April 2004: invalid care allowance, statutory sick pay and statutory maternity or paternity pay paid by the Inland Revenue or taxable incapacity benefit.

Where to find the information

Your benefit office will have given you a statement or form showing the amount payable and, where applicable, the taxable portion of the benefit.

● Invalid Care Allowance	**11.6**	£
● Statutory Payments paid by the Inland Revenue *including Statutory Sick, Maternity, Paternity and Adoption Pay*	**11.7**	£
	Tax deducted	Gross amount **before** tax
● Taxable Incapacity Benefit	**11.8** £	**11.9** £

What to enter

State the taxable amount received or due to you for the year ended 5 April 2004 in the relevant box. In the case of incapacity benefit, the Department for Work and Pensions will give you a form advising of the tax position. (It is not taxable for the first 28 weeks of incapacity or if paid when incapacity began before 13 April 1995 and for which invalidity benefit used to be payable.)

Statutory sick pay, maternity or paternity pay should only be shown if paid direct to you by the Inland Revenue; if it was paid to you by your employer then it will be included on your P60 or P45 form and you would declare these in the Employment pages of the tax return (see page 39).

Do not include

Any additional allowances for a dependant child as that is tax free.

> **Tax tip** Tax back on pensions
> If you receive a pension in addition to the State pension it is possible you may be able to claim some tax back (see page 78).

Other pensions and retirement annuities 11.10 – 11.14

Fill this in if

You received a UK pension other than the State pension between 6 April 2003 and 5 April 2004.

Where to find the information

At the end of each tax year, the company paying you the pension or annuity must send you a P60 form (see page 80) or a statement by 31 May 2004.

■ *Other pensions and retirement annuities*

● Pensions (other than State pensions) and retirement annuities - *if you have more than one pension or annuity, please add together and complete boxes 11.10 to 11.12. Provide details of each one in box 11.14*

Amount after tax deducted	Tax deducted	Gross amount **before** tax
11.10 £	**11.11** £	**11.12** £

11.14

● Deduction - *see the note for box 11.13 on page 15 of your Tax Return Guide*

Amount of deduction
11.13 £

What to enter

The gross amount received from a personal pension scheme, any income withdrawals in respect of a deferred annuity and annual payments from a retirement contract in the year ended 5 April 2004 should be shown in 11.12 and the total of any tax deducted in 11.11. (Box 11.10 is 11.12 less the amount in 11.11.)

Certain pensions are exempted in whole or part from UK tax, in which case enter the amount in box 11.13. If you have received more than one pension enter details in box 11.14.

Use the tax organiser on page 100 if you have several pensions so that you can add them together.

Do not include

Pensions received from abroad – these go in the Foreign section of your tax return (see page 63).

Q12 Other income

This section covers less familiar forms of income which will not apply to the majority of taxpayers. If you have received any of these listed in boxes 12.1 to 12.12 tick the 'Yes' box and fill in the information requested.

If not, then move on to Q13 overleaf.

 Q12 **Did you make any gains on UK life insurance policies, life annuities or capital redemption policies or receive refunds of surplus funds from additional voluntary contributions?**   **YES** | **If yes**, tick this box and then fill in boxes 12.1 to 12.12 as appropriate. If not applicable, go to Question 13.

Other income 12.1 – 12.12

Fill this in if

You made gains on UK annuities, life insurance policies or those in ISAs that have been made void, or you received a repayment from a AVC pension scheme.

Where to find the information

The insurance company or scheme's trustees will have given you a statement containing the figures.

• Gains on UK annuities and friendly societies' life insurance policies where no tax is treated as paid	Number of years **12.1**			Amount of gain(s) **12.2** £
• Gains on UK life insurance policies etc. on which tax is treated as paid - *read pages 15 to 18 of your Tax Return Guide*	Number of years **12.3**	Tax treated as paid **12.4** £		Amount of gain(s) **12.5** £
• Gains on life insurance policies in ISAs that have been made void	Number of years **12.6**	Tax deducted **12.7** £		Amount of gain(s) **12.8** £
• Corresponding deficiency relief	Amount **12.9** £			
• Refunds of surplus funds from additional voluntary contributions	Amount received **12.10** £	Notional tax **12.11** £		Amount plus notional tax **12.12** £

What to enter

In the case of life policies, the relevant number of years, notional tax and amounts received as shown on the insurance company's statement; for AVC refunds, the amounts received and notional tax figures.

Q13 Miscellaneous income

If you received any other income not covered so far in your tax return, then tick the 'Yes' box. Such income could include casual earnings, mail-order commission, royalties, lump sums from unapproved retirement benefits schemes, post-cessation receipts, taxable cash-backs from mortgage companies, etc. If not, then move on to Q14.

Q13 **Did you receive any other taxable income which you have not already entered elsewhere in your Tax Return?**
Fill in any supplementary Pages before answering Question 13.
(Supplementary Pages follow page 10, or are available from the Orderline.)
Or go to www.inlandrevenue.gov.uk

YES ☐

If yes, tick this box and then fill in boxes 13.1 to 13.6 as appropriate.
If not applicable, go to Question 14.

Other taxable income 13.1 – 13.6

Fill this in if
You received any miscellaneous income not declared anywhere else in your tax return or you have losses to be recorded.

The notes attached to your tax return give a long list of the types of income that may be entered here and their tax treatment.

Where to find the information
Statements, receipts, invoices, contract notes, etc.

- Other taxable income – also provide details in box 23.5 - *read the notes on pages 18 to 20 of your Tax Return Guide*

	Amount **after** tax deducted	Tax deducted	Amount **before** tax
	13.1 £	**13.2** £	**13.3** £

- Tick box 13.1A if box 13.1 includes enhanced capital allowances for environmentally friendly expenditure

	Losses brought forward	Earlier years' losses used in 2003-04
13.1A ☐	**13.4** £	**13.5** £

2003-04 losses carried forward
13.6 £

What to enter
The amount received in the year ended 5 April 2004 *after* claiming any allowable expenses (see page 43).

If tax has been deducted this must be shown. If you have losses brought forward, or you are creating a loss in this year, then these amounts must also be shown. If necessary, you may add further details in the additional information box 23.5.

Use the tax organiser sheets on page 100 to summarise your totals.

Tax tip Casual income
You will have entered most of your income in other sections or under the Employment or Land & Property pages. Casual income you received should only be shown *after* you have deducted business expenses incurred in securing that income so you are declaring a net 'profit'. You may have incurred a net loss on miscellaneous activities in which case if the loss cannot be offset against other miscellaneous income or 'profit', you can carry it forward (box 13.4) and use it against miscellaneous income next year.

The above only applies to 'activity' income. You cannot offset expenses against income that has arisen from such sources as an unapproved retirement scheme. .

Post-cessation receipts can be taxed in the year in which the business ceased, in which case don't complete this section but tick box 23.4 (see page 35).

Q14 Relief for pension contributions

If you are a member of your employer's pension scheme and no other scheme and all your contributions have been deducted at source, then ignore this section and move on to Q15. (You will get tax relief on these contributions deducted under PAYE.) Tick the 'Yes' box if you want to claim relief for other pension-scheme contributions.

Q14	**Do you want to claim relief for your pension contributions?** **YES** ☐	**If yes,** tick this box and then fill in boxes 14.1 to 14.11 as appropriate. If not applicable, go to Question 15.

Do not include contributions deducted from your pay by your employer to their pension scheme or associated AVC scheme, because tax relief is given automatically. But *do include* your contributions to personal pension schemes and Free-Standing AVC schemes.

Retirement annuity contracts 14.1 – 14.5

Fill this in if
You have made contributions to a retirement annuity contract and/or you wish to allocate payments to a different tax year.

Where to find the information
Your insurance company will provide a certificate of payments at the end of each year.

■ *Payments to your retirement annuity contracts - only fill in boxes 14.1 to 14.5 for policies taken out before 1 July 1988.*
See the notes on pages 20 and 21 of your Tax Return Guide.

Qualifying payments made in 2003-04	**14.1** £	2003-04 payments used in an earlier year	**14.2** £	Relief claimed box 14.1 *minus* (boxes 14.2 and 14.3, but not 14.4)
2003-04 payments now to be carried back	**14.3** £	Payments brought back from 2004-05	**14.4** £	**14.5** £

What to enter
The amounts paid in the year ended 5 April 2004. There are boxes to complete if you wish to carry back pension contributions, have already allocated payments to an earlier year, or wish to bring back payments already paid after 5 April 2004.

Tax tip Claiming relief
As there is great flexibility with retirement annuity contracts to allocate contributions over different years to give you the most advantageous tax benefit, you will find it useful to use the tax organiser on page 100 of this book so you can keep a record of the amounts you have paid each year and the amounts carried back to other years. After all, you can claim any unused relief going back over six years.

You have until 31 January 2005 to decide if you want to allocate any payment made in the year ended 5 April 2004 to the previous year. If you make a payment after you have sent in your tax return ask the Inland Revenue for claim form 43.

Personal pensions and stakeholder pensions 14.6 – 14.9

Fill this in if
You have made contributions to a personal or stakeholder pension scheme.

Where to find the information
Your insurance company will provide a certificate of payments at the end of each tax year.

■ *Payments to your personal pension (including stakeholder pension) contracts* - enter the amount of the payment you made with the basic rate tax added (the **gross** payment). See the note for box 14.6 on page 22 of your Tax Return Guide.

Gross qualifying payments made in 2003-04	**14.6** £	
2003-04 gross payments carried back to 2002-03	**14.7** £	Relief claimed
		box 14.6 minus box 14.7 (but not 14.8)
Gross qualifying payments made between 6 April 2004 and 31 January 2005 brought back to 2003-04 - *see page 22 of your Tax Return Guide*	**14.8** £	**14.9** £

What to enter
The amounts you have contributed to personal and/or stakeholder pensions in the year ended 5 April 2004 and your claim to carry back any payments to the previous tax year. Tax at basic rate will have been deducted from the premium when you paid it, so you need to add the tax deducted to the net amount and show the gross amount in your tax return.

Do not include
Contributions deducted from your salary by your employer to an occupational pension scheme. You will already have had tax relief under PAYE as shown on your P60 form (and recorded in box 1.8 under the Employment supplementary sheets).

Tax tip Carry-back payments
You must advise your pension provider and the Inland Revenue on forms PP43 and PPP120 if you wish to carry back payments, and remember that any payment made between 6 April 2004 and 31 January 2005 can be carried back to the tax year ended 5 April 2004, up to your maximum allowance (see table on page 103).

Tax tip Pension contributions
If you have paid personal pension contributions in excess of the maximum allowance for the year to 5 April 2004, you cannot carry forward unused reliefs if you have paid less than maximum contributions in the previous six years. Under Stakeholder pension rules, you can contribute up to £3,600 to a personal pension plan even if you have no earnings, and you will still get tax relief. You can choose your earnings from either the current year or one of the previous five tax years as a basis for calculating the maximum contribution you can pay to a personal pension. You can, therefore, continue to pay contributions at a level determined by your basis year for up to five years after the income has ceased, after which time you will be limited to a contribution of £3,600. For personal pension plans taken out after 14 March 1989 the maximum net relevant earnings figures on which relief is available are: £95,400 for 2001–2002, £97,200 for 2002–2003, £99,000 for 2003–2004 and £102,000 for 2004–2005.

Other pension contributions 14.10 – 14.11

Fill this in if

You have made a contribution to an employer's scheme which has not been deducted from your salary, e.g. an additional voluntary contribution (14.10), any amount paid as a top up to a free-standing additional voluntary contribution scheme (14.11).

Where to find the information

Your insurance company or scheme manager will provide you with a certificate of payments at the end of each tax year.

■ *Contributions to other pension schemes and Free-Standing AVC schemes*

● Amount of contributions to employer's schemes **not deducted** at source from pay **14.10** £

● Gross amount of Free-Standing Additional Voluntary Contributions paid in 2003-04 **14.11** £

What to enter

The gross amount of the contributions made.

> **Tax tip** Stakeholder v AVCs
> It can be more beneficial to top up your pension fund by taking out a Stakeholder pension rather than making free-standing additional voluntary contributions to an employer's scheme because under a Stakeholder scheme you can take a tax-free lump sum on retirement – this is not so with AVCs.

Q15 Other reliefs you can claim

This section covers an extensive assortment of reliefs.
Tick the 'Yes' box if you want to claim for interest paid on qualifying loans, certain maintenance and alimony payments or Child Support Agency payments if either you or your wife or husband were born before 5 April 1935; also claim under this section for Venture Capital Trust and Enterprise Investment Scheme subscriptions, gifts of money or investments made to charities, post-cessation expenses, annuities or payments to a trade union or friendly society for death benefits or to your employer for a compulsory benefits scheme for widows, widowers or orphans.
If you do not need to claim any of these reliefs go to Q15A on page 25.

Q15 **Do you want to claim any of the following reliefs?**
If you have made any annual payments, after basic rate tax, answer 'Yes' to Question 15 and fill in box 15.9. If you have made any gifts to charity go to Question 15A.

 YES

If yes, tick this box and then fill in boxes 15.1 to 15.12, as appropriate.
If not applicable, go to Question 15A

Interest paid on qualifying loans 15.1

Fill this in if
You pay interest on a loan which was used to buy shares in, or lend to:
- a closely controlled trading company where you own more than 5 per cent of the company's shares, or, if less, have worked for the greater part of your time in the management of the company – such interest is not allowed for tax if a claim for relief has been made under the Enterprise Investment Scheme;
- a partnership or employee-controlled company;
- a co-operative, provided that you work in it full time.

Or you pay interest on a loan to buy plant or machinery for business use.

Or you pay interest on a loan to buy an annuity if the person buying the annuity was aged 65 or over, the loan was secured on the individual's main residence in the UK or Republic of Ireland, and the loan was taken out before 9 March 1999 (or other loans have replaced the original loan). Relief for these loans is restricted to 22 per cent up to a maximum loan of £30,000.

You can request help sheet IR340 for more information about what you can claim.

There is also an Inland Revenue helpline – 0151 472 6155.

Where to find the information
Ask the lender for a certificate of interest from which you can obtain the figures to go in your return.

Amount of payment

- Interest eligible for relief on qualifying loans **15.1** £

What to enter
The gross amount actually paid, but there is no need to enter a figure in respect of loan interest to buy an annuity if relief has been given under MIRAS.

Do not include
Any interest in box 15.1 on a loan to purchase let property; this should be entered in box 5.26 in the Land and Property return (see page 61).

Interest on loans to buy your main home is no longer allowed as a tax deduction.

Maintenance or alimony payments 15.2 – 15.2A

Fill this in if
You, or your former husband or wife, were born before 6 April 1935 and you make legally enforceable maintenance or alimony payments. Relief is only available at 10 per cent.

Where to find the information
You will know the payments made from your own records or from a court, DWP or Child Support Agency statement.

- Maintenance or alimony payments you have made under a court order, Child Support Agency assessment or legally binding order or agreement

Amount claimed up to £2,150

| 15.2 | £ |

To claim this relief, either you or your former spouse must have been 65 or over on 5 April 2000. So, if **your** date of birth, which is entered in box 22.6, is after 5 April 1935 then you must enter your former **spouse's** date of birth in box 15.2A - *see pages 23 and 24 of your Tax Return Guide*

Former spouse's date of birth

| 15.2A | / | / |

What to enter
In box 15.2 state the lower of the amount you paid in the year ended 5 April 2004 or £2,150, as the maximum figure for tax relief is only £2,150.

If your former husband or wife has remarried in 2003–2004 the relief ceases from the date of the marriage.

Do not include
Voluntary payments for there is no tax relief for these.

Venture capital trusts, etc. 15.3 – 15.7

Fill this in if
You have subscribed for shares in a Venture Capital Trust or an Enterprise Investment Scheme (EIS) or made investments in a community development finance institution (CDFI).

Where to find the information
The trust or scheme will have given you a share certificate and a memorandum of the trust's status, etc. and a receipt for the amount paid.

You will receive a form EIS3 or EIS5 for EIS investments, which the tax office may wish to see to support your claim.

For CDFI, the institution will give you a certificate covering your investment.

- Subscriptions for Venture Capital Trust shares (up to £100,000)

Amount on which relief is claimed

| 15.3 | £ |

- Subscriptions under the Enterprise Investment Scheme (up to £150,000) - *also provide details in box 23.5, see page 24 of your Tax Return Guide*

Amount on which relief is claimed

| 15.4 | £ |

- Community Investment Tax relief - invested amount relating to previous tax year(s) and on which relief is due

| 15.5 | £ |

Total amount on which relief is claimed

box 15.5 + box 15.6

- Community Investment Tax relief - invested amount for current tax year

| 15.6 | £ |

| 15.7 | £ |

What to enter
The amount you subscribed up to the maximum. For EIS subscriptions you will also need to enter the name of the company, subscription on which relief is claimed, date of issue of the shares and the Inland Revenue office which authorised the issue and their reference number in the additional information box 23.5 on page 9 of your return.

With CDFIs, the amounts you invested. Relief will be at 5 per cent per year of the amount you lend or invest for up to five years.

Trading cessation, etc. 15.8

Fill this in if
You ceased trading within the last seven years but have still incurred expenditure closely related to that business, or you have losses carried forward from self-employment and you transfer your business to a company. Losses on discounted securities are also entered here.

Where to find the information
From invoices, receipts, correspondence, etc.

	Amount of payment
• Post-cessation expenses, pre-incorporation losses brought forward and losses on relevant discounted securities, etc. - *see pages 24 and 25 of your Tax Return Guide*	**15.8** £

What to enter
The amount of the relevant expenditure.

> **Tax tip** Relief on capital losses
> If your income in the year of payment of certain post-cessation expenses is not sufficient to utilise the relief fully, then a claim may be made for the excess to be treated as an allowable loss for capital gains tax purposes (see page 70).

Annuities paid 15.9

Fill this in if
You have paid annuities or covenants for genuine commercial reasons in connection with your trade or profession.

Where to find the information
Annuity statements or copies of the covenant form.

	Payments made
• Annuities and annual payments	**15.9** £

What to enter
The amount actually paid in the year ended 5 April 2004. These payments are treated as having been made after basic rate tax has been deducted – further relief will only be due if you are a higher-rate taxpayer.

Do not include
Covenants to individuals for non-trade or professional reasons. No tax relief is available on these.

Trade union or friendly society payments 15.10

Fill this in if
Part of your trade union subscription relates to a pension, insurance or funeral benefit, or you have a friendly society policy providing sickness and death benefits (the part relating to death benefit may qualify for tax relief). Most friendly society policies no longer qualify for this relief.

Where to find the information
The society or trade union operating the policies will provide you each year with a statement that will give you the figures required.

	Half amount of payment
• Payments to a trade union or friendly society for death benefits	15.10 £

What to enter
One half of the payment made relating to superannuation, life assurance, funeral or death benefit.

Payments to employer's benefit scheme 15.11

Fill this in if
You had to make compulsory payments to your employer's compulsory widow's, widower's or orphan's benefit scheme and relief has not already been given under PAYE.

Where to find the information
The statement from your employer or the scheme's trustees.

	Relief claimed
• Payment to your employer's compulsory widow's, widower's or orphan's benefit scheme - *available in some circumstances – first read the notes on page 25 of your Tax Return Guide*	15.11 £

What to enter
The lower of either £100 or 22 per cent of the amount not relieved under PAYE.

Redemption of bonus shares, etc. 15.12

Fill this in if
You received bonus shares or securities and you are a higher rate taxpayer who has entered income from redeeming shares in box 10.17 of your tax return.

Where to find the information
The contract notes or offer document.

	Relief claimed
• Relief claimed on a qualifying distribution on the **redemption** of bonus shares or securities.	15.12 £

What to enter
This is a very complicated calculation. Refer to the tax return guide notes. Ring orderline 0845 9000 404 if you do not have a copy.

Q15A Claiming tax relief on gifts to charity

If you have made gifts to charities either by covenants, gift aid schemes or a donation of shares or property tick the 'Yes' box and fill in the required information.

If this section does not apply to you, then turn to Q16 on page 27.

Q15A **Do you want to claim relief on gifts to charity?**
If you have made any Gift Aid payments answer 'Yes' to Question 15A. You should include Gift Aid payments to Community Amateur Sports Clubs here. You can elect to include in this Return Gift Aid payments made between 6 April 2004 and the date you send in this Return. See page 26 in the Tax Return Guide.

 YES [ ]

If yes, tick this box and then read page 26 of your Tax Return Guide. Fill in boxes 15A.1 to 15A.7 as appropriate.
If not applicable, go to Question 16.

Gifts of cash to charities 15A.1 – 15A.5

Fill this in if

You have signed a covenant prior to 6 April 2000 to pay money to a charity for a period of at least four years OR you have donated money to a charity and signed a Gift Aid certificate R190(SD).

Where to find the information

You should have a copy of the covenant form you signed, or a note of the cash payments made for which you have given an appropriate declaration to the charity.

- Gift Aid payments, including covenanted payments to charities, made between 6 April 2003 and 5 April 2004

  15A.1 £

- Enter in box 15A.2 the total of any 'one off' payments included in box 15A.1

  15A.2 £

- Enter in box 15A.3 the amount of Gift Aid payments made after 5 April 2003 but treated as if made in the tax year 2002-03

  15A.3 £

- Enter in box 15A.4 the amount of Gift Aid payments made after 5 April 2004 but treated as if made in the tax year 2003-04

  15A.4 £

- Enter in box 15A.5 the total relief claimed in 2003-04

  box 15A.1 + box 15A.4 minus box 15A.3
  15A.5 £

What to enter

In boxes 15A.1 and 15A.2 the net amounts actually paid. You will be regarded as having deducted tax at basic rate before making the payments, so further tax relief is only available if you are a higher-rate taxpayer. The tax office will assume that any one-off payments are not on-going when assessing your tax code.

In box 15A.3, enter the net amount of payments which have already been treated as paid in the previous tax year.

In box 15A.4, enter the net amount of Gift Aid payments made between 5 April 2004 and the date you submit your tax return (no later

than 31 January 2005) for you can carry back these payments to the previous year and get tax relief earlier than would otherwise be the case.

Do not include

Details of charitable donations made via a payroll giving scheme.

Tax tip Gift aid and non-taxpayers
Non-taxpayers should not sign any gift aid form as you cannot claim tax relief; if you do, you will have to refund the tax that has been claimed by the charity.

Gifts of investments or property to charities 15A.6 – 15A.7

Fill this in if
You have gifted qualifying shares, unit trusts or property to a UK charity or you have sold them to a charity for less than their market value.

Where to find the information
Contract notes transferring the shares or investments. Freehold or leasehold contract notes.

You must get a certificate from the charity confirming that they have accepted your gift.

● Gifts of qualifying investments to charities – shares and securities	**15A.6** £	
● Gifts of qualifying investments to charities – real property	**15A.7** £	

What to enter
The total value, at the time of transfer, of all the investments or property given or sold to charities in the year ended 5 April 2004, including any costs involved (brokers' fees, stamp duty, etc.) in making the gift. You must deduct any consideration or value actually received by you, if any.

Tax tip Gifts to charity
If you are contemplating making a gift of shares or property to a charity and you are already making a profit on them, then it would be more tax-efficient if you gave the assets discreetly to the charity rather than selling them first. It would also benefit the charity more, tax-wise.

Q16 Your tax allowances for the year ending 5 April 2004

You automatically get the personal allowance each year if you are resident in the UK but all other allowances have to be claimed.

If you want to claim the blind person's allowance or married couple's allowance, then tick the 'Yes' box. Otherwise, proceed to Q17, but don't forget to enter your age in box 22.6 on page 9 of your return – if you were born before 6 April 1939 you may be entitled to a higher personal allowance.

 Do you want to claim blind person's allowance, or married couple's allowance?
You get your personal allowance of £4,615 automatically.
If you were born before 6 April 1939, enter your date of birth in box 22.6
- you may get a higher age-related personal allowance.

If yes, tick this box and then read pages 26 to 28 of your Tax Return Guide. Fill in boxes 16.1 to 16.17 as appropriate.
If not applicable, go to Question 17.

Blind person's allowance 16.1 – 16.2

Fill this in if
You are a registered blind person.

	Date of registration (if first year of claim)	Local authority (or other register)
■ *Blind person's allowance*	**16.1** / /	**16.2**

What to enter
The date you were registered blind if it is the first time you have claimed, and also the name of your local authority.

Residents of Scotland or Northern Ireland may not be registered with the local authority and should enter either 'Scotland claim' or 'Northern Ireland claim'.

Tax tip **Blind person's allowance**
This allowance is also claimable by blind persons in the year *preceding* the year in which they were officially registered as blind if, at the end of the previous year, evidence was *then* available to support the eventual registration application. This allowance is transferable to a husband or wife even if he or she is not blind (see page 29).

Married couple's allowance 16.3 – 16.13

Fill this in if

Either you, or your husband or wife, were born before 6 April 1935. (If both of you were born after this date, you cannot claim the married couple's allowance.)

> ### Tax tip The age-allowance trap
> If you are married, over 65 and claiming age allowance, estimate your total income for the next tax year to see that no personal allowance will remain unused; it may be beneficial to transfer savings, etc. into joint names. See page 97 for income limits.

> ### Tax tip Who gets the married couple's allowance?
> The allowance automatically goes to the husband unless either the husband or the wife has asked for one half to be given to each other (box 16.7 or 16.10) or both husband and wife have asked for the whole allowance to be given to the wife (boxes 16.8 and 16.11).
>
> With the abolition of the married couple's allowance from 6 April 2000 for younger couples, this allowance will only apply to those couples where either the husband or wife was aged 65 or over on or before 5 April 2000.
>
> It is beneficial to transfer this allowance if it cannot be used fully by a husband. Ask your tax office for Form 18 if you wish to transfer half, or all, of the married couple's allowance, but this has to be submitted before the tax year to which it relates so it is already too late for it to apply to the 2004–2005 tax year, but see page 29 regarding surplus allowances.

■ **Married couple's allowance -**

*In 2003-04 married couple's allowance can only be claimed if either you, or your husband or wife, were born **before 6 April 1935**. So you can only claim the allowance in 2003-04 if either of you had reached **65 years of age before 6 April 2000**. Further guidance is given beginning on page 27 of your Tax Return Guide.*

If **both** you and your husband or wife were born after 5 April 1935 you cannot claim; **do not** complete boxes 16.3 to 16.13.

If you can claim fill in boxes 16.3 and 16.4 if you are a married man or if you are a married woman and you are claiming half or all of the married couple's allowance.

- Enter your date of birth (if born before 6 April 1935) — **16.3** / /

- Enter your spouse's date of birth (**if born before 6 April 1935 and** if older than you) — **16.4** / /

Then, if you are a married man fill in boxes 16.5 to 16.9. If you are a married woman fill in boxes 16.10 to 16.13.

- Wife's full name **16.5** _____ | • Date of marriage (if after 5 April 2003) **16.6** / /

- Tick box 16.7, or box 16.8, if you or your wife have allocated half, or all, of the minimum amount of the allowance to her — Half **16.7** | All **16.8**

- Enter in box 16.9 the date of birth of any previous wife with whom you lived at any time during 2003-04. *Read 'Special rules if you are a man who married in the year ended 5 April 2004' on page 28 before completing box 16.9.* — **16.9** / /

- Tick box 16.10, or box 16.11, if you or your husband have allocated half, or all, of the minimum amount of the allowance to you — Half **16.10** | All **16.11**

- Husband's full name **16.12** _____ | • Date of marriage (if after 5 April 2003) **16.13** / /

What to enter

Your date of birth in 16.3 and your wife or husband's date of birth, if older than you, in 16.4.

If you are a married man fill in boxes 16.5 to 16.9 with ticks or date of birth – married women should similarly fill in boxes 16.10 to 16.13.

Transfer of surplus allowances 16.14 – 16.17

Fill this in if

You are unable to use all your married couple's allowance or blind person's allowance and wish to transfer the surplus to your husband or wife.

■ **Transfer of surplus allowances** - *see page 28 of your Tax Return Guide before you fill in boxes 16.14 to 16.17.*

● Tick box 16.14 if you want your spouse to have your unused allowances 　　　**16.14**

● Tick box 16.15 if you want to have your spouse's unused allowances 　　　**16.15**

Please give details in the 'Additional information' box, box 23.5, on page 9 - *see page 28 of your Tax Return Guide for what is needed.*

If you want to calculate your tax, enter the amount of the surplus allowance you can have.

● Blind person's surplus allowance 　　　**16.16** £

● Married couple's surplus allowance 　　　**16.17** £

What to enter

If you have surplus allowances to transfer, tick the appropriate box.

You may also add your calculation of the surplus allowances available in boxes 16.16 to 16.17 if you wish to calculate your own tax liability.

Q17 Student loan repayment

Repayment of student loans made to a new borrower since August 1998 is now collected via the tax system. These loans are called 'Income Contingent'. Tick the 'Yes' box if the Student Loans company told you that repayment commenced before 6 April 2004. Otherwise, move on to Q18.

 Are you liable to make Student Loan Repayments for 2003-04 on an Income Contingent Student Loan?
You must read the note on page 29 of your Tax Return Guide before ticking the 'Yes' box.

 If yes, tick this box.
If not applicable, go to Question 18.

Q18 Do you want to calculate your own tax?

If you *do not* want to calculate your own tax liability or tax refund and you would prefer the tax office to do it for you, go on to Q19.

If you *do* want to do it yourself, then tick 'Yes' and complete the boxes as shown.

Q18	**Do you want to calculate your tax and, if appropriate, any Student Loan Repayment?**	**YES** ☐	Use your Tax Calculation Guide then fill in boxes 18.1 to 18.8 as appropriate.

Calculating your own tax 18.1 – 18.8

Fill this in if
You want to calculate your own tax.

• Underpaid tax for earlier years included in your tax code for 2003-04	**18.1** £
• Underpaid tax for 2003-04 included in your tax code for 2004-05	**18.2** £
• Student Loan Repayment due	**18.2A** £
• Class 4 NIC due	**18.2B** £
• Total tax, Class 4 NIC and Student Loan Repayment due for 2003-04 **before** you made any payments on account *(put the amount in brackets if an overpayment)*	**18.3** £
• Tax due calculated by reference to earlier years - *see the notes on page 10 of your Tax Calculation Guide (SA151W)*	**18.4** £
• Reduction in tax due calculated by reference to earlier years - *see the notes on page 10 of your Tax Calculation Guide (SA151W)*	**18.5** £
• Tick box 18.6 if you are claiming to reduce your 2004-05 payments on account. Make sure you enter the **reduced** amount of your first payment in box 18.7. Then, in the 'Additional information' box, box 23.5 on page 9, say why you are making a claim	**18.6** ☐
• Your first payment on account for 2004-05 *(include the pence)*	**18.7** £
• Any 2004-05 tax you are reclaiming now	**18.8** £

What to enter
You need to turn to page 88 of this book for a tax calculation summary, then you can complete boxes 18.1 to 18.8.

Q19 Do you want to claim a tax repayment

If you are due a tax repayment of more than £10 and you *don't* want it offset against your next tax bill, or through your PAYE code number, then tick 'Yes' and fill in the information requested. If you do not claim a repayment but one is due to you, then the tax office will set any amount to be refunded against your next tax bill. Now proceed to Q19A.

 Do you want to claim a repayment if you have paid too much tax? *(If you do not tick 'Yes' or the tax you have overpaid is below £10, I will use the amount you are owed to reduce your next tax bill.)*

If yes, tick this box. Then, if you want to nominate all or part of your repayment to charity, go to Question 19A; if you want to claim a repayment, go to Question 19B.

If not applicable, go to Question 20.

Tax tip Checking your PAYE code
There may be many reasons why you are due a tax repayment – it may be due to a claim for gift aid or an additional pension contribution – but if it was due to the fact that you have had the wrong PAYE code number, then do make sure that the tax office alter your code once they have processed your tax return, otherwise you will continue to overpay tax in the next year.

Q19A Nominate any repayment to a charity

Any tax repayment due to you can be nominated to a charity of your choice. If this is your wish then tick the 'Yes' box. If not, proceed to Q19B.

Q19A **Do you want to nominate a charity to receive all or part of your repayment?** *See page 29 of your Tax Return Guide and the leaflet enclosed on Gift Aid.*

YES ☐

If yes, tick this box and then read page 29 of your Tax Return Guide. Fill in boxes 19A.1 to 19A.5 as appropriate.
If not applicable, go to Question 19B.

Tax repayment to a charity 19A.1 – 19A.5

Fill this in if
You want to nominate a charity to receive all or part of your tax repayment.

Where to find the information
From your own records and tax return details.

- Tick box 19A.1 if you want to nominate a charity to receive **all** of your repayment   **19A.1** ☐

- If you want to nominate a charity to receive part of your repayment, enter the amount in box 19A.2
  – if you want the remainder of your repayment to be paid to you or your nominee, you must fill in Question 19B   **19A.2** £ ☐

- Charity code – *enter the Charity code in box 19A.3. You can get the Charity code by visiting www.inlandrevenue.gov.uk, ringing the Helpline on 0845 9000 444 or by contacting your local Inland Revenue office*   **19A.3** ☐☐☐☐☐ **G**

- Tick box 19A.4 if you wish Gift Aid to apply and are making the declaration below   **19A.4** ☐

- Tick box 19A.5 to confirm we can provide the charity with details of your name and address when we notify them of your donation   **19A.5** ☐

Gift Aid declaration – I want my gift to the nominated charity to be treated as a Gift Aid donation. The charity will receive basic rate income tax on my gift. I confirm that I will pay at least as much income or capital gains tax in 2004-05 as the charity will receive on my donation.

What to enter
Decide whether you want to donate all your tax refund to a charity (19A.1) or part of your refund (19A.2). Put the charity code in 19A.3 – if you do not know this, telephone the helpline on 0845 302 0203.

If you are a taxpayer then tick 19A.4 and 19A.5 confirming that the gift is covered by the Gift Aid rules so that the charity can reclaim the tax.

> **Tax tip Gift aid and non-taxpayers**
> If you are not a taxpayer you should not sign any gift aid form as you cannot claim tax relief on tax that you haven't paid; if you do the Inland Revenue will ask you to refund the tax that has effectively been claimed by the charity.

Q19B Where do you want your repayment paid?

If you have ticked 'Yes' in Q19, and you don't want to donate your refund to charity, tick 'Yes' in Q19B; otherwise proceed to Q20.

Q19B Do you want your repayment to be paid to yourself or to your nominee?

YES If yes, tick this box and then fill in boxes 19B.1 to 19B.14 as appropriate.
If not applicable, go to Question 20.

Where do you want your repayment paid? 19B.1 – 19B.14

Fill this in if

You want your tax repayment made to your bank or building society account or to a nominee.

Repayments will be sent direct to your bank or building society account. This is the safest and quickest method of payment. If you do not have an account, tick box 19B.8. If you would like repayment to your nominee, tick box 19B.2 or 19B.9.

Should the repayment be sent:

- to **your** bank or building society account? *Tick box 19B.1 and fill in boxes 19B.3 to 19B.7* **19B.1**

or

- to **your** nominee's bank or building society account? *Tick box 19B.2 and fill in boxes 19B.3 to 19B.7 and 19B.11 to 19B.14* **19B.2**

- If you do not have a bank or building society account, read the notes on page 29, *tick box 19B.8* **19B.8**

- If you would like a cheque to be sent to your nominee, *tick box 19B.9 and fill in boxes 19B.11 to 19B.14* **19B.9**

- If your nominee is your agent, *tick box 19B.10* **19B.10**

Name of bank or building society

19B.3

Name of account holder

19B.4

Branch sort code

19B.5

Account number

19B.6

Building society reference

19B.7

Agent's reference for you (if your nominee is your agent)

19B.11

I authorise
Name of your nominee/agent

19B.12

Nominee/agent address

19B.13

Postcode

to receive on my behalf the amount due

19B.14 *This authority must be signed by you. A photocopy of your signature will not do.*

Signature

What to enter

Your bank, building society or agent's details.

Q20 Have you received a tax refund?

Tick the 'Yes' box if you have received a tax refund from the tax office or benefits agency in the year ended 5 April 2004, or notification of any refund reallocated to other tax liabilities (including CIS25 deductions) and state the amount.

Q20 **Have you already had any 2003-04 tax refunded or set off by your Inland Revenue office or the Benefits Agency (in Northern Ireland, the Social Security Agency)?**
Read the notes on page 30 of your Tax Return Guide.

YES | If yes, tick this box and then enter the amount of the refund in box 20.1.

20.1 £

Q21 and Q22 Check your personal details

Check your name, address and reference number on the front page of your tax form, if correct, then proceed to Q22; if wrong, tick Q21 and correct the details on the front page of the return. You do not *have* to state a telephone number but it could save the tax office and you having to write letters to sort out a minor problem or misunderstanding.

Q21 **Is your name or address on the front of the Tax Return *wrong*?**
If you are filling in an approved substitute Tax Return, see the notes on page 30 of the Tax Return Guide.

YES | If yes, please tick this box and make any corrections on the front of the form.

Q22 **Please give other personal details in boxes 22.1 to 22.7.** *This information helps us to be more efficient and effective.*

Your daytime telephone number
22.1

Your agent's telephone number
22.2

and their name and address
22.3

Postcode

Your first two forenames
22.4

Say if you are single, married, widowed, divorced or separated
22.5

Your date of birth (If you were born before 6 April 1939, you may get a higher age-related personal allowance.)
22.6 / /

Your National Insurance number
(if known and not on page 1 of your Tax Return)
22.7

Q23 Additional information

Your tax office needs all this additional information in order to ensure that your tax affairs are dealt with efficiently; if there is insufficient room, use the additional information box at 23.5.

Q23 ▶ **Please tick boxes 23.1 to 23.4 if they apply. Provide any additional information in box 23.5 below (continue on page 10, if necessary).**

Tick box 23.1 if you do **not** want any tax you owe for 2003-04 collected through your tax code.

23.1

Please tick box 23.2 if this Tax Return contains figures that are provisional because you do not yet have final figures. Pages 32 and 33 of the Tax Return Guide explain the circumstances in which provisional figures may be used and asks for some additional information to be provided in box 23.5 below.

23.2

Tick box 23.3 if you are claiming relief now for 2004-05 trading, or certain capital, losses. Enter in box 23.5 the amount and year.

23.3

Tick box 23.4 if you are claiming to have post-cessation or other business receipts taxed as income of an earlier year. Enter in box 23.5 the amount and year.

23.4

23.5 *Additional information*

Q24 Declaration

You must sign and date the declaration, ensuring that you have ticked the boxes to indicate which sections of the tax return you have completed and, where appropriate, enter the number of sets of supplementary pages you are returning.

Q24 **Declaration**

I have filled in and am sending back to you the following pages:

Tick

*In the second box enter the number of **complete sets** of supplementary Pages enclosed*

	Tick	Number of sets		Tick	Number of sets		Tick
1 TO 10 OF THIS FORM							
EMPLOYMENT			**PARTNERSHIP**			**TRUSTS, ETC**	
SHARE SCHEMES		Number of sets	**LAND & PROPERTY**			**CAPITAL GAINS**	
SELF-EMPLOYMENT			**FOREIGN**			**NON-RESIDENCE, ETC**	

Before you send your completed Tax Return back to your current Inland Revenue office, you must sign the statement below. If you give false information or conceal any part of your income or chargeable gains, you may be liable to financial penalties and/or you may be prosecuted.

24.1 The information I have given in this Tax Return is correct and complete to the best of my knowledge and belief.

Signature

Date

There are very few reasons why we accept a signature from someone who is not the person making this Return but if you are signing for someone else please read the notes on page 31 of the Tax Return Guide, and:

- enter the capacity in which you are signing (for example, as executor or receiver)

24.2

- enter the name of the person you are signing for

24.3

- please **PRINT** your name and address in box 24.4

24.4

Postcode

Tax tip Sign your tax return
Many tax returns, particularly those being sent in after 30 September last year, were unsigned and this means that the return is wrongly submitted and not complete. This could waste time and cost you interest and penalties. Make sure you sign it!

Tax tip Keeeping records
With self assessment tax legislation, the law requires you to keep all records of earnings, income, benefits, profits, expenses, etc. and all other relevant information for 22 months from the end of the tax year if you are employed, and for five years and 10 months if you are self-employed.

When you have completed your tax return

Sign the return and keep a copy

When you sign your tax return you are declaring that to the best of your knowledge and belief the return is complete, true and accurate.

It is often thought that if you keep quiet about some of your income, then the tax inspector will not find out about it. This is not the case. The tax authorities have many sources of information, the most common being your employer, banks, building societies and other businesses, all of whom may be required to make a return of payments made to individuals and businesses. If you forget to include some of your income on the form you should immediately notify your tax office explaining your error.

You should keep a copy of your completed tax return form so that, at a later date, you can check your PAYE code or the amount of tax you have paid. If you fill in the tax forms reproduced in this book you will have a permanent record.

Keep your own records

You will only have entered total figures in the boxes on your tax return, so ensure that you keep a note of how you arrived at the figures – the tax office may ask for them. Use the tax organiser at the end of this book.

When to send in your tax return if you don't want to calculate your own tax

You need to send in your tax return by 30 September 2004 – the tax office should then send you a statement by 31 January 2005. This form, SA302 'Self assessment – Tax Calculation for 2003–2004' will either agree your figures or identify corrections that the tax office have made. If you disagree with the tax office's comments write to them; otherwise pay the amount demanded. If you file your tax return on-line then your tax will automatically be calculated for you.

When to send in your tax return if you want to calculate your own tax

If you wish to use the tax calculator and calculate your own tax liability (see page 88) then you have until 31 January 2005 to send in your return, in which case you should also pay the tax that you think is due.

If you miss the return date

If you send in your return after 30 September 2004 (and you don't want to calculate your own tax) the tax office will not guarantee to calculate it for you before 31 January; they will still send you, however, a demand for a payment on 31 January, so you need to know approximately what your tax liability is in total.

> **Tax tip** Claiming allowances
> Do not worry if you have forgotten to claim an allowance due to you, for you have a time limit of six years in which to tell your tax office of your mistake. Therefore you can go back to 6 April 1997 to check your tax and possibly get a rebate – and interest too.

Payments on account

If you have enough untaxed income, or are self-employed, you will have to make two payments on account for each tax year, e.g. for the year ended 5 April 2004, the first payment for 50 per cent of your expected tax bill on 31 January 2004, and the second 50 per cent on 31 July 2004; any balance due once your tax liability is agreed is payable on 31 January 2005. If there is a tax refund due, your tax office will deal with it fairly quickly. (Self-employed payments will also include Class 4 National Insurance liability.) It is up to you to work out how much you need to pay on account, although your tax office will normally send you an 'on account' statement once your pattern of income is established.

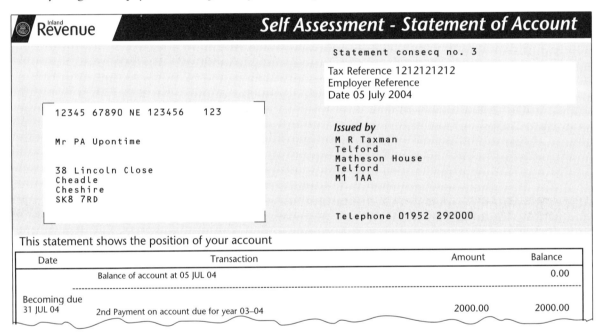

Inland Revenue

Self Assessment - Statement of Account

Statement consecq no. 3

Tax Reference 1212121212
Employer Reference
Date 05 July 2004

12345 67890 NE 123456   123

Mr PA Upontime

38 Lincoln Close
Cheadle
Cheshire
SK8 7RD

Issued by
M R Taxman
Telford
Matheson House
Telford
M1 1AA

Telephone 01952 292000

This statement shows the position of your account

Date	Transaction	Amount	Balance
	Balance of account at 05 JUL 04		0.00
Becoming due 31 JUL 04	2nd Payment on account due for year 03–04	2000.00	2000.00

What to do with this form

Form SA300 above is an example of a demand for payment of tax – either on account or for a specific tax liability. If you agree with the figure, you should pay the amount by the date shown otherwise you could incur interest payments (see page 5). If it is wrong, ask for form SA303 (below).

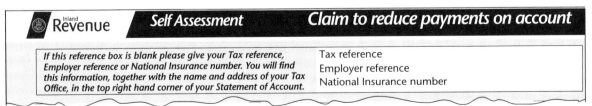

Inland Revenue   *Self Assessment*   **Claim to reduce payments on account**

If this reference box is blank please give your Tax reference, Employer reference or National Insurance number. You will find this information, together with the name and address of your Tax Office, in the top right hand corner of your Statement of Account.

Tax reference
Employer reference
National Insurance number

Fill this in if

You wish to reduce the amount of tax and National Insurance being demanded on account. You must fill in the appropriate boxes on this form so that the tax office understands why you are claiming a reduction.

Send the completed form to your tax office, together with a cheque for the revised payment on account that you calculate is due. If the claim to reduce is excessive and you have a liability at the end of the tax year, then interest will be payable from the original date.

Your tax return – supplementary pages

Q1 Employment

If you were employed during the tax year you will have ticked the 'Yes' box on page 2 of your tax return and you will need to fill in these supplementary pages where applicable. You must use a separate form for each employment. Ministers of Religion and MPs have different versions of this form.

Employment income 1.1 – 1.11

Fill this in if

You are an employee or a director, and receive a salary, wages, fees or benefits or you are an agency worker (but not an entertainer or working exclusively from home).

Where to find the information

By law, your employer has to give you a P60 form (certificate of pay, income tax and National Insurance) by 31 May 2004 (see page 80). This will show the earnings figures to go in your tax return, and the tax deducted. Alternatively, you may need to refer to a P45 form or your pay slips.

Details of employer

Employer's PAYE reference - may be shown under 'Inland Revenue office number and reference' on your P60 or 'PAYE reference' on your P45

1.1 _____

Employer's name

1.2 _____

Date employment started
(only if between 6 April 2003 and 5 April 2004)

1.3 ___ / ___ / ___

Employer's address

1.5 _____

Date employment finished
(only if between 6 April 2003 and 5 April 2004)

1.4 ___ / ___ / ___

Tick box 1.6 if you were a director of the company

1.6 ____

and, if so, tick box 1.7 if it was a close company

1.7 ____

Postcode

Income from employment

■ **Money** - see Notes, page EN3

● Payments from P60 (or P45)

Before tax

1.8 £ ____

● Payments not on P60, etc.   - tips

1.9 £ ____

     - other payments (excluding expenses entered below and lump sums and compensation payments or benefits entered overleaf)

1.10 £ ____

● **Tax deducted** in the UK from payments in boxes 1.8 to 1.10

Tax deducted

1.11 £ ____

What to enter

Fill in boxes 1.1 to 1.7 with the information requested. In box 1.8 show the amount you have received *before* any deductions for income tax or National Insurance. You *are* allowed to subtract any deduction made by your employer for contributions to an approved pension scheme, payroll giving donations or lump sum leaving payment (see page 41). Enter in box 1.9 any tips received if they are not included in box 1.8. Box 1.10 is for any other payments, although most of them will be specifically referred to later in this form. Enter any tax deducted in box 1.11.

Employment benefits 1.12 – 1.23

Fill this in if

You have received any benefits from your employer. Typically those might include private health cover or a low-interest loan.

Your employer has provided you, or your family, with a car available for your private use.

Your employer has either paid directly or reimbursed any expenses relating to your employment, not covered by a dispensation.

Where to find the information

Most of the information will be found on the P11D or P9D form, a copy of which your employer must give you by 6 July 2004. For an explanation of how car and fuel benefits are calculated, see page 83.

	Amount		Amount
• Assets transferred/ payments made for you	**1.12** £	• Vans	**1.18** £
• Vouchers, credit cards and tokens	**1.13** £	• Interest-free and low-interest loans *see Note for box 1.19, page EN5*	**1.19** £
• Living accommodation	**1.14** £	box 1.20 is not used	
• Excess mileage allowances and passenger payments	**1.15** £	• Private medical or dental insurance	**1.21** £
• Company cars	**1.16** £	• Other benefits	**1.22** £
• Fuel for company cars	**1.17** £	• Expenses payments received and balancing charges	**1.23** £

What to enter

The amount paid to you as a benefit or expense or the taxable value.

If your employer has agreed with the tax office that certain expenses need not be shown as you would be entitled to tax relief for the full amount (e.g. representatives' overnight stays; mileage allowances for your own car used on business), then your employer should give you details of the expenses covered by the arrangement.

Tax tip Tax on benefits and expenses
All directors and those employees whose earnings, including expenses and benefits in kind, are at a rate of £8,500 or more a year are liable to pay tax on benefits and expenses received.

Certain benefits are taxable on all employees – some are tax free.

The car benefit tax applies to all company cars, including those that are leased.

Refer to page 86 for more information.

Compensation and lump sums 1.24 – 1.30A

Fill this in if

You have been made redundant or dismissed with compensation; you have received a lump sum under the terms of your contract of employment; you have received payments from an unapproved retirement scheme.

Where to find the information

You will find the information in a letter or statement from your employer; or from the trustees of an unapproved retirement scheme.

■ *Lump sums and compensation payments or benefits including such payments and benefits from a former employer*
Note that 'lump sums' here includes any contributions which your employer made to an unapproved retirement benefits scheme

You must read page EN6 of the Notes *before* filling in boxes 1.24 to 1.30

Reliefs

- £30,000 exception — **1.24** £
- Foreign service and disability — **1.25** £
- Retirement and death lump sums — **1.26** £

Taxable lump sums

- From box B of *Help Sheet IR204* — **1.27** £
- From box K of *Help Sheet IR204* — **1.28** £
- From box L of *Help Sheet IR204* — **1.29** £
- Tax deducted from payments in boxes 1.27 to 1.29 - *leave blank if this tax is included in the box 1.11 figure and tick box 1.30A.* — Tax deducted **1.30** £
- Tick this box if you have left box 1.30 blank because the tax is included in the box 1.11 figure — **1.30A**

What to enter

As this is a complicated subject you may need Inland Revenue help sheet IR204 to assist you in filling in these boxes. If it has not been sent, then telephone 0845 9000 404 for a copy.

Do not include

A tax figure in box 1.30 if the tax is included in the figures on your P60 form entered in box 1.10 on page 39; you will need to tick box 1.30A to confirm this.

> **Tax tip** Is your compensation taxable?
> The first £30,000 of compensation is tax free but any amount in excess of that figure is taxable at your highest individual rate of tax. Note that if your contract of employment gives you a right to compensation on ceasing to be employed, then any lump sum you receive will be taxable, regardless of the amount.

Foreign non-taxable earnings 1.31

Fill this in if
You are non-resident (see page 75) or have reason to believe such foreign income is not liable to UK tax.

Where to find the information
From your financial accounts and records.

■ Foreign earnings not taxable in the UK in the year ended 5 April 2004 - see Notes, page EN6	**1.31** £

What to enter
That part of your income that you think is not taxable in the UK.

> **Tax tip** Tax status
> Status will depend on whether you are resident or ordinarily resident and your domicile. Refer to help sheet IR211 available from Inland Revenue offices or from their website at
> www.inlandrevenue.gov.uk

Expenses claimed – travel and subsistence 1.32

Fill this in if
Your employer has reimbursed your business expenses incurred or you have paid an expense that has not been reimbursed, without which you would have been unable to do your job properly (the law says the expense must be 'wholly, exclusively and necessary for your employment').

Where to find the information
From your financial accounts and records.

■ Expenses you incurred in doing your job - see Notes, pages EN7 to EN8	
● Travel and subsistence costs	**1.32** £

What to enter
The amount of the expense, after taking into account the 'tax tip' comments. Any shortfall between the actual payment received and the Inland Revenue mileage allowance can be claimed here.

Do not include
Travel costs incurred from your home to your *permanent* place of business – they are regarded as being personal mileage. The form asks you to tick box 1.36 (see later) if you *have* included personal mileage, but be prepared to explain why you have claimed this amount.

> **Tax tip** Travel expenses
> Bear in mind that unless your employer had a dispensation, then the expenses received will have already been declared in 1.23 (on page 40) – here you are in effect 'claiming' them as a legitimate deduction. Get a letter from your employer confirming these facts.
> If you are travelling on business and are away from home you can claim accommodation, meals, etc.

Fixed deductions for expenses 1.33

Fill this in if
Your trade union has agreed with the tax inspector a fixed allowance that can be claimed to cover certain expenses (e.g. engineers £45 to £120 a year, agricultural workers £70 a year). Alternatively, keep a record of your actual 'business' expenses and submit an annual claim under box 1.35.

Healthcare workers similarly have a scale of fixed allowances agreed with their representatives.

Where to find the information
From your financial accounts and records.

• Fixed deductions for expenses	**1.33** £	

What to enter
The fixed sum agreed with your trade union.

Professional fees and subscriptions 1.34

Fill this in if
You paid a fee or subscription to an organisation of which you are a member or to whom a payment was requested as a condition of your job. The organisation must be on the approved Inland Revenue list.

Where to find the information
From your financial accounts and records.

• Professional fees and subscriptions	**1.34** £	

What to enter
The relevant fee or subscription total.

Other expenses claimable 1.35 – 1.36

Fill this in if
You have incurred other expenses that were necessary for your employment – see tax tip – or if you used equipment for your work that you had provided (e.g. a computer) you can claim capital allowances.

Where to find the information
From your financial accounts and records.

> **Tax tip** Expenses you can claim
> Apart from those expenses referred to in the form, under 1.35 you could consider claiming for: protective clothing and laundering costs; trade journals and technical books; the cost of business mileage travelled using your own car, bicycle or motorbike – see page 84; use of a room at home as an office based on a proportion of your costs if you *have* to do additional work at home.

• Other expenses and capital allowances	**1.35** £	
• Tick box 1.36 if the figure in box 1.32 includes travel between your home and a permanent workplace	**1.36**	

What to enter

The total of the relevant expenses – use the tax organiser on page 104 to add up your individual expenses.

(As regards 1.36 see the notes under 1.32.)

See page 51 for details of capital allowance rates.

Do not include

Claims for capital allowances for a motor vehicle provided by yourself for business use. This has not been an allowable expense since 2002. Such cost is considered to be included in any mileage allowance.

Foreign earnings declaration 1.37 – 1.38

Fill this in if

You are a seafarer or you do not want to claim tax credit relief.

Where to find the information

The rules are very complicated so ask your tax office for help sheet IR2055 by ringing 0845 9000 444.

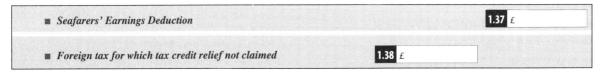

- *Seafarers' Earnings Deduction*   **1.37** £
- *Foreign tax for which tax credit relief not claimed*   **1.38** £

What to enter

The relevant amounts as defined in the help sheets issued with your tax return.

Student loan repayments 1.39 – 1.40

Fill this in if

You had student loan repayments deducted by your employer.

Where to find the information

Your P60 form, and pay slips from previous employer(s) if you had more than one job.

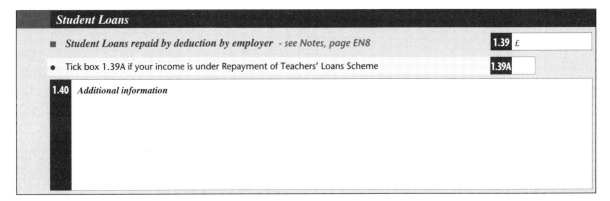

Student Loans

- *Student Loans repaid by deduction by employer* - see Notes, page EN8   **1.39** £
- Tick box 1.39A if your income is under Repayment of Teachers' Loans Scheme   **1.39A**

1.40 *Additional information*

What to enter

The amount of loan repayment deducted from your earnings in the year.

Q2 Share options

If you have unapproved share options, or approved share options which have been forfeited or the rules breached, then you will have ticked the 'Yes' box on page 2 of your tax return and will need to fill in these supplementary pages where applicable.

(You need to fill in boxes 2.43 – 2.76 *before* 2.1 – 2.42.)

Share option schemes

The tax legislation governing share schemes generally has grown out of all proportion with each succeeding budget and this section now runs to three pages. Because of their complexity, it is not possible to simplify the numerous rules and regulations covering every type of scheme.

You will need to fill in boxes 2.43 – 2.76 *before* you do the summary sheet 2.1 – 2.42 and you will need a separate copy of pages S2 or S3 for each taxable event.

Remember that you do not need to fill in these share option supplementary sheets if your scheme is approved by the Inland Revenue and you have not breached any of the regulations.

Schemes can vary considerably from employer to employer, and before filling in this part of the tax return you should ask for Inland Revenue help sheet IR 218 – telephone 0845 9000 404 if you require a copy – and also seek guidance from the trustees of your share scheme or your employer.

If you have made any capital gains or losses, do not enter them in this section – ask the tax office for Capital Gains supplementary pages by telephoning order line 0845 9000 404.

Share options 2.43 – 2.52

Fill this in if

You have been granted share options in an unapproved scheme (or you have forfeited share options in an approved scheme or broken one of the Inland Revenue rules (see page 45).

Where to find the information

Share option certificates, correspondence or exercise notes. Your employer should give you details of any taxable event.

	Name of company and share scheme	Class of share (for example, 10p Ordinary)
2.43		**2.44**

		Options granted	Options exercised	Options cancelled/released
2.45	Date option was granted	/ /	/ /	/ /
2.46	Date option was exercised		/ /	
2.47	Number of shares			
2.48	Exercise price: option price per share	£ .	£ .	
2.49	Amount, if any, paid for grant of option	£ .	£ .	£ .
2.50	Market value per share at date the option was granted	£ .		
2.51	Market value per share at date the option was exercised		£ .	
2.52	Amount received in money or money's worth			£ .

Enterprise management incentive options 2.53 – 2.63

Fill this in if
You have been granted an enterprise management incentive option at a discounted price or failed to exercise the option within 40 days of a disqualifying event occurring.

Where to find the information
Contract notes for discontinued options or details from your employer if a disqualifying event occurred.

	Name of company and unique option reference	Class of share (for example, 10p Ordinary)
2.53		**2.54**

		Options exercised	Options cancelled/released
2.55	Date option was granted	/ /	/ /
2.56	Date of disqualifying event	/ /	
2.57	Number of shares		
2.58	Exercise price: option price per share	£ .	
2.59	Amount, if any, paid for grant of option	£ .	£ .
2.60	Market value per share at date the option was granted	£ .	
2.61	Market value per share at date of the disqualifying event	£ .	
2.62	Market value per share at date the option was exercised	£ .	
2.63	Amount received in money or money's worth		£ .

Approved share incentive plans 2.64 – 2.68

Fill this in if
The shares issued under an approved share incentive plan cease to be covered by the rules laid down by the Inland Revenue (for example if you change your job within five years of the original acquisition).

Where to find the information
Share certificates and/or correspondence from your employer.

	Name of company and share plan	Class of shares (for example 10p Ordinary)
2.64		**2.65**

2.66	Date shares ceased to be subject to the plan	/ /
2.67	Market value per share when shares ceased to be subject to the plan	£ .
2.68	Number of shares	

Securities acquired 2.69 – 2.75

Fill this in if
You acquire shares or securities from your employment which were not obtained via an approved profit sharing scheme or share option or you have received certain benefits as a consequence of owning shares.

Where to find the information
Share certificates and/or correspondence from your employer.

2.69 Name of company and securities scheme	**2.70** Type of security (for example, 10p Ordinary share)

	Securities acquired	Post-acquisition (event)
2.71 Date securities acquired or post-acquisition event	/ /	/ /
2.72 Number of securities		
2.73 Amount paid per security	£ .	
2.74 Market value per security at date of acquisition or post-acquisition event	£ .	£ .
2.75 Give details of the nature of the post-acquisition event		

Income tax paid 2.76

Fill this in if
Your employer has deducted tax on the grant of your option (or if for some reason you have paid tax directly on the grant of an option).

Where to find the information
Tax deduction certificate from your employer.

- Income Tax paid on the grant of your option   **2.76** £

2.77 *Additional information*

Share options (summary) 2.1 – 2.42

Fill this in if
You have made any entries on pages S2 or S3 covered in boxes 2.43 to 2.77.

Where to find the information
Entries made in pages S2 or S3 on this return. Ensure you follow the instructions in the tax notes accompanying this return and the working sheets.

■ *Approved savings-related share options*

		Name of company and share scheme	Tick if shares unlisted	Taxable amount
• Exercise	**2.1**		**2.2**	**2.3** £
• Cancellation or release	**2.4**		**2.5**	**2.6** £

■ *Approved discretionary share options*

		Name of company and share scheme		
• Exercise	**2.7**		**2.8**	**2.9** £
• Cancellation or release	**2.10**		**2.11**	**2.12** £

■ *Enterprise Management Incentive options*

		Name of company and unique option reference		
• Exercise	**2.13**		**2.14**	**2.15** £
• Cancellation or release	**2.16**		**2.17**	**2.18** £

■ *Unapproved securities options*

		Name of company and securities scheme		
• Grant	**2.19**		**2.20**	**2.21** £
• Exercise	**2.22**		**2.23**	**2.24** £
• Cancellation or release	**2.25**		**2.26**	**2.27** £

Approved Share Incentive Plans

*Read the Notes on page SN2 **before** filling in the boxes*

		Name of company and share plan	
• Shares ceasing to be subject to the plan	**2.28**		**2.29**	**2.30** £

Continue filling this column, as appropriate, and make sure you fill in boxes 2.40 and 2.42

Securities acquired

*Read the Notes on page SN8 **before** filling in the boxes*

		Name of company and securities scheme		
• Securities acquired from your employment	**2.31**		**2.32**	**2.33** £
• Securities as benefits	**2.34**		**2.35**	**2.36** £
• Post-acquisition events	**2.37**		**2.38**	**2.39** £

■ *Totals*

		total column above
• Total of the taxable amounts boxes (total boxes in the right-hand column, starting with box 2.3)		**2.40** £
• Any taxable amounts included in boxes 2.6 to 2.39 which are included in the Pay figure on your P60 or P45(Part 1A)		**2.41** £
		box 2.40 *minus* box 2.41
Total taxable amount		**2.42** £

Q3 Self-employment

If you were self-employed at any time during the tax year you will have ticked the 'Yes' box on page 2 of your tax return and you will need to fill in these supplementary pages where applicable. (If you were in a partnership, then you need the Partnership supplementary pages – see page 57.)

Telephone the Inland Revenue order line on 0845 9000 404 if you need either of these forms – you need to fill in a separate set of pages for each business.

Business details 3.1 – 3.13

Fill this in if
You had income from work done on a self-employed or freelance basis, or you let furnished rooms and provided services so that it was considered as a 'trade'. Do not fill in these pages if you were trading as a partnership (see introduction above).

Where to find the information
From your financial accounts and records.

Name of business
3.1

Description of business
3.2

Address of business
3.3

Postcode

Accounting period - *read the Notes, page SEN2 before filling in these boxes*

Start
3.4 / /

End
3.5 / /

- Tick box 3.6 if details in boxes 3.1 or 3.3 have changed since your last Tax Return
  3.6

- Date of commencement if after 5 April 2001
  3.7 / /

- Date of cessation if before 6 April 2004
  3.8 / /

- Tick box 3.9 if the special arrangements for certain trades apply - *read the Notes, pages SEN11 and SEN12*
  3.9

- Tick box 3.10 if you entered details for all relevant accounting periods on last year's Tax Return and boxes 3.14 to 3.73 and 3.99 to 3.115 will be blank *(read Step 3 on page SEN2)*
  3.10

- Tick box 3.11 if your accounts do not cover the period from the last accounting date (explain why in the 'Additional information' box, box 3.116)
  3.11

- Tick box 3.12 if your accounting date has changed (only if this is a permanent change and you want it to count for tax)
  3.12

- Tick box 3.13 if this is the second or further change (explain in box 3.116 on Page SE4 why you have not used the same date as last year)
  3.13

What to enter
State the kind of work you do and your business name and address (it may be your normal name or a trading name) and fill in boxes 3.4 and 3.5 with the relevant dates, and tick 3.6 to indicate any changes.

Boxes 3.10 to 3.13 need ticking where relevant – they are designed to let the tax office know of any change in your business accounting dates. Fill in box 3.7 if you have started in business since 5 April 2001, and fill in 3.8 if you have ceased trading before 6 April 2004.

Capital allowances 3.14 – 3.23

Fill this in if

You wish to claim capital allowances – regardless of your turnover level.

Where to find the information

From your financial accounts and records.

	Capital allowances	Balancing charges
• Cars costing more than £12,000 (excluding cars with low CO² emissions) (A separate calculation must be made for each car.)	**3.14** £	**3.15** £
• Other business plant and machinery (including cars with low CO² emissions and cars costing less than £12,000) *read the Notes, page SEN4*	**3.16** £	**3.17** £
• Agricultural or Industrial Buildings Allowance (A separate calculation must be made for each block of expenditure.)	**3.18** £	**3.19** £
• Other capital allowances claimed (Separate calculations must be made.)	**3.20** £	**3.21** £
Total capital allowances/balancing charges	total of column above **3.22** £	total of column above **3.23** £
• Tick box 3.22A if box 3.22 includes enhanced capital allowances for environmentally friendly expenditure	**3.22A**	

What to enter

Any depreciation shown in your accounts will have been added back as disallowable in assessing your profit for tax purposes (see page 53); instead you can claim capital allowances as set out in the table below. (A balancing charge arises if you sell an asset for more than its tax written-down value – that is its original cost less cumulative capital allowances claimed.)

Table of capital allowances for 2003–2004

Allowances	First year capital allowance From 2 July 1998 %	Writing down % on reducing balance thereafter %
Plant, machinery and equipment★	40†	25
Fixtures and fittings	40†	25
Motor cars (maximum £3,000 a year)	–	25
Vans and lorries	40†	25
Office furniture and equipment	40†	25
Insulation of factories and warehouses	40†	25
Fire safety expenditure	40†	25
	From 1 April 2000 to 31 March 2004	
Computer hardware and software, high-tech mobile phones and internet set-top boxes (For small businesses only)‡	100	
	From 1 April 2001	
Energy saving plant and machinery – all businesses	100	
Creating flats over shops for letting	100	
	From 17 April 2002	
Low-emission or electric cars (new) and refuelling equipment	100	on cost
Factories and warehouses	–	4
Agricultural buildings	–	4
Hotel buildings	–	4
Houses under assured tenancies scheme	–	4

Notes:
There are higher allowances for buildings in enterprise zones, scientific research and film production expenditure, and special provisions for patent rights, know how, mines, mineral rights and certain other assets; also 150 per cent tax credits from 1 April 2000 for research and development.
★ The annual rate of writing down allowance will be reduced to 6 per cent for most assets with a working life of 25 years or more purchased, or contracted, on or after 26 November 1996, but this applies only to businesses which spend more than £100,000 a year on such assets.
† Only applies to small to medium-sized businesses (see below). There are higher rates for Northern Ireland.
‡ Small businesses are defined as having an annual turnover of not more than £2.8 (5.6) million, assets not exceeding £1.4 (2.8) million with a maximum of 50 employees. The figures for medium-sized businesses are £11.2 (22.8) million, £5.6 (11.4) million and 250 employees respectively. Two out of three of these conditions must be met. The figures in brackets apply to financial years ending on or after 30 January 2004.

Turnover less than £15,000 a year? 3.24 – 3.26

Fill this in if
Your business turnover is less than £15,000 a year.

Where to find the information
From your financial accounts and records.

---

*If your annual turnover is £15,000 or more, **ignore** boxes 3.24 to 3.26. Instead fill in Page SE2* ➤

*If your annual turnover is below £15,000, **fill in boxes 3.24 to 3.26 instead of Page SE2**. Read the Notes, page SEN2.*

- Turnover including other business receipts and goods etc. taken for personal use (and balancing charges from box 3.23) **3.24** £

- Expenses allowable for tax (including capital allowances from box 3.22) **3.25** £

box 3.24 *minus* box 3.25

Net profit (put figure in brackets if a loss) **3.26** £

What to enter
You only need to give three figures: your turnover, allowable expenses and profit (or loss). Obviously you will have prepared your own accounts in order to obtain these figures.

It is not necessary to send your accounts to the tax office with your tax return but you must keep them so that you can answer any queries that they may arise.

Do not fill this in if
Your miscellaneous income from self-employment is from a one-off freelance or spare-time activity. You should declare this income under Miscellaneous Income (see page 17 of this book).

Having filled in this section, now turn to box 3.74 (page 54 in this book), or if your turnover is *more* than £15,000 fill in the following sections.

Turnover more than £15,000 a year? 3.27 – 3.65

Fill this in if
Your business turnover is *more* than £15,000 a year.

Where to find the information
From your financial accounts and records.

	Disallowable expenses included in boxes 3.46 to 3.63	Total expenses	
If you were registered for VAT, do the figures in boxes 3.29 to 3.64, include VAT? **3.27** ☐ or exclude VAT? **3.28** ☐			Sales/business income (turnover) **3.29** £
Cost of sales	**3.30** £	**3.46** £	
Construction industry subcontractor costs	**3.31** £	**3.47** £	
Other direct costs	**3.32** £	**3.48** £	box 3.29 *minus* (boxes 3.46 + 3.47 + 3.48)
		Gross profit/(loss)	**3.49** £
		Other income/profits	**3.50** £
Employee costs	**3.33** £	**3.51** £	
Premises costs	**3.34** £	**3.52** £	
Repairs	**3.35** £	**3.53** £	

• General administrative expenses	**3.36** £		**3.54** £		
• Motor expenses	**3.37** £		**3.55** £		
• Travel and subsistence	**3.38** £		**3.56** £		
• Advertising, promotion and entertainment	**3.39** £		**3.57** £		
• Legal and professional costs	**3.40** £		**3.58** £		
• Bad debts	**3.41** £		**3.59** £		
• Interest	**3.42** £		**3.60** £		
• Other finance charges	**3.43** £		**3.61** £		
• Depreciation and loss/(profit) on sale	**3.44** £		**3.62** £		
• Other expenses	**3.45** £		**3.63** £		

Put the total of boxes 3.30 to 3.45 in box 3.66 below

	total of boxes 3.51 to 3.63
Total expenses	**3.64** £

	boxes 3.49 + 3.50 *minus* 3.64
Net profit/(loss)	**3.65** £

What to enter

Not all the expenditure shown in your financial accounts will be allowable for tax against profits, which is why there are two columns of figures – the left-hand column (3.30 to 3.45) identifying any amounts that are disallowable; the figures to go in the right-hand column (3.46 to 3.63) are those shown in your accounts.

Turnover more than £15,000 a year? (continued) 3.66 – 3.73

Fill this in if

Your business turnover is *above* £15,000 a year and you have completed boxes 3.27 to 3.65.

Where to find the information

From your financial accounts and records.

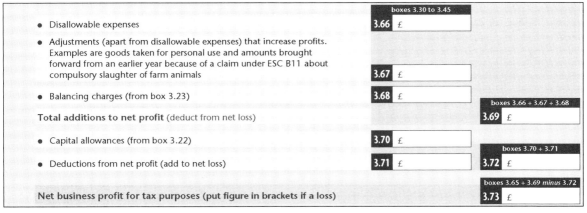

	boxes 3.30 to 3.45
• Disallowable expenses	**3.66** £
• Adjustments (apart from disallowable expenses) that increase profits. Examples are goods taken for personal use and amounts brought forward from an earlier year because of a claim under ESC B11 about compulsory slaughter of farm animals	**3.67** £
• Balancing charges (from box 3.23)	**3.68** £
Total additions to net profit (deduct from net loss)	boxes 3.66 + 3.67 + 3.68 **3.69** £
• Capital allowances (from box 3.22)	**3.70** £
• Deductions from net profit (add to net loss)	**3.71** £ boxes 3.70 + 3.71 **3.72** £
Net business profit for tax purposes (put figure in brackets if a loss)	boxes 3.65 + 3.69 *minus* 3.72 **3.73** £

What to enter

The total disallowable expenses (box 3.66) shown above; an estimate of goods, etc. used personally (box 3.67). Box 3.68 is for any balancing charge (see page 51); Box 3.70 totals your capital allowances (see page 51); Box 3.71 is for any amounts included in your accounts which are either not taxable or not relevant to your business, although it is more likely that you will have covered these in the disallowable items on the previous page. Include any compulsory slaughter relief in box 3.71.

Calculating your taxable profit 3.74 – 3.93

Fill this in if
You have completed any of the sections of these supplementary pages so far, regardless of your turnover level.

Where to find the information
From your financial accounts and records.
There is an Inland Revenue helpline for newly self-employed people – 0845 915 4515.

Adjustments to arrive at taxable profit or loss

Basis period begins **3.74** / / and ends **3.75** / /

Profit or loss of this account for tax purposes (box 3.26 or 3.73) **3.76** £

Adjustment to arrive at profit or loss for this basis period **3.77** £

- Overlap profit brought forward **3.78** £   • Deduct overlap relief used this year **3.79** £

- Overlap profit carried forward **3.80** £

Averaging for farmers and creators of literary or artistic works *(see Notes, page SEN9, if you made a loss for 2003-04)* **3.81** £

Adjustment on change of basis **3.82** £

Net profit for 2003-04 (if you made a loss, enter '0') **3.83** £

Allowable loss for 2003-04 (if you made a profit, enter '0') **3.84** £

- Loss offset against other income for 2003-04 **3.85** £

- Loss to carry back **3.86** £

- Loss to carry forward (that is allowable loss not claimed in any other way) **3.87** £

- Losses brought forward from earlier years **3.88** £

- Losses brought forward from earlier years used this year **3.89** £

Taxable profit after losses brought forward   box 3.83 *minus* box 3.89 **3.90** £

- Any other business income (for example, Business Start-up Allowance received in 2003-04) **3.91** £

Total taxable profits from this business   box 3.90 + box 3.91 **3.92** £

- Tick box 3.93 if the figure in box 3.92 is provisional **3.93**

What to enter
The totals (where applicable) from boxes completed on previous pages. (Ask for help sheet IR222 from your tax office.)

Note also that there are special tax rules governing new businesses and those that have ceased trading.

Tax tip National insurance
As well as coping with keeping account books and records and the tax implications generally, self-employed people must understand how the National Insurance system works, otherwise you could have arrears of debt to pay, or find yourself unable to claim certain exemptions or benefits.

National insurance contributions 3.94 – 3.96

Fill this in if

You are claiming exemption or deferment from Class 4 NICs; or you have a 'cash basis' adjustment or trading losses brought forward. These NI payments are based on 8 per cent of your taxable profit (after deducting capital allowances, but including any enterprise allowance received) between £4,615 and £30,940 and 1 per cent over £30,940.

Where to find the information

From your financial accounts and records.

Class 4 National Insurance contributions - see Notes, page SEN10		
• Tick box 3.94 if exception applies	**3.94**	
• Tick box 3.95 if deferment applies	**3.95**	
• Adjustments to profit chargeable to Class 4 National Insurance contributions	**3.96** £	

What to enter

Tick box 3.94 if you are exempted from Class 4 NICs and write in any adjustment in boxes 3.95 and 3.96.

> **Tax tip** Exemption or deferment
> Reasons for exemption or deferment may be due to your age, profit levels or infirmity. Ask for leaflet CA72.

Subcontractors in the construction industry 3.97

Fill this in if

You are a subcontractor in the construction industry and have received any payments under that industry's tax deduction scheme.

Where to find the information

From your financial accounts and records.

Subcontractors in the construction industry	
• Deductions made by contractors on account of tax (please send your CIS25s to us)	**3.97** £

What to enter

The total amounts shown on CIS25 vouchers even if you have already claimed repayment of some of the tax. The vouchers should be sent in with your tax return.

Tax deducted from trading income 3.98

Fill this in if

Any tax has been deducted from your trading income (other than by subcontractors). An example would be tax deducted from overseas royalty income.

Where to find the information

From your financial accounts and records.

Tax deducted from trading income	
• Any tax deducted (excluding deductions made by contractors on account of tax) from trading income	**3.98** £

Summary of balance sheet 3.99 – 3.116

Fill this in if

Your turnover is over £15,000 and you are submitting a balance sheet with your profit and loss account. If you are not submitting a balance sheet leave these boxes blank.

Where to find the information

From your financial accounts and records.

Summary of balance sheet

▶ Leave these boxes blank if you do not have a balance sheet

- **Assets**
  - Plant, machinery and motor vehicles — **3.99** £
  - Other fixed assets (premises, goodwill, investments etc.) — **3.100** £
  - Stock and work-in-progress — **3.101** £
  - Debtors/prepayments/other current assets — **3.102** £
  - Bank/building society balances — **3.103** £
  - Cash in hand — **3.104** £

  total of boxes 3.99 to 3.104 — **3.105** £

- **Liabilities**
  - Trade creditors/accruals — **3.106** £
  - Loans and overdrawn bank accounts — **3.107** £
  - Other liabilities — **3.108** £

  total of boxes 3.106 to 3.108 — **3.109** £

- **Net business assets** (put the figure in brackets if you had net business liabilities)

  box 3.105 *minus* 3.109 — **3.110** £

- **Represented by**

  Capital Account
  - Balance at start of period* — **3.111** £
  - Net profit/(loss)* — **3.112** £
  - Capital introduced — **3.113** £
  - Drawings — **3.114** £
  - Balance at end of period* —

  total of boxes 3.111 to 3.113 *minus* box 3.114 — **3.115** £

*If the Capital Account is overdrawn, or the business made a net loss, enter the figure in brackets.

3.116 *Additional information*

What to enter

The figures, suitably grouped, from your accounts.

Q4 Partnerships

If you carried on a business as a partnership during the tax year you will have ticked the 'Yes' box on page 2 of your tax return and you will need to fill in these supplementary pages where applicable.

Partnerships 4.1 – 4.79

Fill this in if

You were entitled to a share of profits, losses or income from a business which you carried on in partnership.

Where to find the information

You will have received a partnership statement or set of accounts for each partnership for which you were a partner and for each business if the partnership carried on more than one business.

Partnership details

Partnership reference number

4.1

Description of partnership trade or profession

4.2

- Date you started being a partner (if during 2003-04) **4.3** / /

- Date you stopped being a partner (if during 2003-04) **4.4** / /

Your share of the partnership's trading or professional income

Basis period begins **4.5** / / and ends **4.6** / /

- Your share of the profit or loss of this year's account for tax purposes (enter a loss in brackets) **4.7** £

- Adjustment to arrive at profit or loss for this basis period **4.8** £

- Overlap profit brought forward **4.9** £   Deduct overlap relief used this year **4.10** £

- Overlap profit carried forward **4.11** £

- Averaging for farmers and creators of literary or artistic works (see Notes, page PN3 if the partnership made a loss in 2003-04) or foreign tax deducted, if tax credit relief not claimed **4.12** £

- Adjustment on change of basis **4.12A** £

What to enter

There are two types of Partnership pages – the short version (shown here) and the long version. Most partnerships will use the short version as their only partnership income will be trading income or taxed income from banks, deposit takers, etc. and these pages summarise information from the partnership return. All partners are jointly responsible for completing the partnership tax return.

You need to complete separate Partnership pages for each business. Some of the information requested is similar to that covered under the self-employed section (see page 50).

Net profit for 2003-04 (if loss, enter '0' in box 4.13 and enter the loss in box 4.14)	**4.13**	£

Allowable loss for 2003-04 — **4.14** £

- Loss offset against other income for 2003-04 — **4.15** £

- Loss to carry back — **4.16** £

- Loss to carry forward
  (that is, allowable loss not claimed in any other way) — **4.17** £

- Losses brought forward from last year — **4.18** £

- Losses brought forward from last year used this year — **4.19** £

Taxable profit after losses brought forward — box 4.13 *minus* box 4.19 **4.20** £

- Add amounts **not** included in the partnership accounts that are needed to calculate your taxable profit (for example, Enterprise Allowance (Business Start-up Allowance) received in 2003-04) — **4.21** £

Total taxable profits from this business — box 4.20 + box 4.21 **4.22** £

Class 4 National Insurance contributions (see Notes, page PN4)

- Tick box 4.23 if exception applies — **4.23**

- Tick box 4.24 if deferment applies — **4.24**

- Adjustments to profit chargeable to Class 4 National Insurance contributions — **4.25** £

Your share of the partnership taxed income

- Share of taxed income (liable at 20%) — **4.70** £

Your share of the partnership trading and professional profits

- Share of partnership profits (other than that liable at 20%) — from box 4.22 **4.73** £

Your share of the partnership tax paid

- Share of Income Tax deducted from partnership income — **4.74** £

- Share of CIS25 deductions — **4.75** £

- Share of tax deducted from trading income (not CIS25 deductions) — **4.75A** £

boxes 4.74 + 4.75 + 4.75A **4.77** £

4.79 *Additional information*

Tax tip Keeping records
All records used to complete the 2003–2004 tax return must be kept until at least 31 January 2010 in case the Inland Revenue wishes to see them.

Q5 Land and property

If you have income under the Rent-a-Room scheme or receive rents from other types of letting, including furnished holiday lettings, you will have ticked the 'Yes' box on page 2 of your tax return and you will need to fill in these supplementary pages where applicable.

Rent-a-room relief

Fill this in if
You wish to claim rent-a-room relief and the gross rents are £4,250 or less a year. (If more, see page 61.)

Where to find the information
From your own accounts and records.

> **Are you claiming Rent a Room relief for gross rents of £4,250 or less?**
> (Or £2,125 if the claim is shared?)
> Read the Notes on page LN2 to find out
> - whether you can claim Rent a Room relief; and
> - how to claim relief for gross rents over £4,250
>
> Yes
>
> If 'Yes', tick box. If this is your only income from UK property, you have finished these Pages

What to enter
Just tick the 'Yes' box if applicable; if you have no other income from land or property you need not complete the rest of the form.

Furnished holiday lettings 5.1 – 5.18

Fill this in if
You have income from furnished holiday lettings in the UK (tick the 'Yes' box).

Where to find the information
From your own accounts and records.

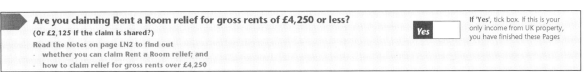

> **Is your income from furnished holiday lettings?**
> If not applicable, please turn over and fill in Page L2 to give details of your property income
>
> Yes
>
> If 'Yes', tick box and fill in boxes 5.1 to 5.18 before completing Page L2

Furnished holiday lettings

- Income from furnished holiday lettings — 5.1 £

Expenses (furnished holiday lettings only)

- Rent, rates, insurance, ground rents etc. — 5.2 £
- Repairs, maintenance and renewals — 5.3 £
- Finance charges, including interest — 5.4 £
- Legal and professional costs — 5.5 £
- Costs of services provided, including wages — 5.6 £
- Other expenses — 5.7 £

total of boxes 5.2 to 5.7
5.8 £

Net profit (put figures in brackets if a loss)

box 5.1 *minus* box 5.8
5.9 £

■ *Tax adjustments*

● Private use   **5.10** £

● Balancing charges   **5.11** £

box 5.10 + box 5.11
5.12 £

● Capital allowances   **5.13** £

● Tick box 5.13A if box 5.13 includes enhanced capital allowances for environmentally friendly expenditure   **5.13A**

Profit for the year (copy to box 5.19). If loss, enter '0' in box 5.14 and put the loss in box 5.15

boxes 5.9 + 5.12 *minus* box 5.13
5.14 £

Loss for the year (if you have entered '0' in box 5.14)

boxes 5.9 + 5.12 *minus* box 5.13
5.15 £

■ *Losses*

● Loss offset against 2003-04 total income   **5.16** £

● Loss carried back
see Notes, page LN4
5.17 £

● Loss offset against other income from property (copy to box 5.38)
see Notes, page LN4
5.18 £

What to enter

The relevant income and expenditure. See page 62 for the types of expenditure you can claim and see page 51 for capital allowance details.

Do not include

Any income from overseas – this should be entered in the Foreign Supplementary pages (see page 63).

Other property income 5.19 – 5.47

Fill this in if

You have other property, or rent-a-room income over £4,250 a year.

Where to find the information

Records of rent received and expenses paid.

Other property income

■ *Income*

● Furnished holiday lettings profits
copy from box 5.14
5.19 £

● Rents and other income from land and property   **5.20** £
Tax deducted
5.21 £

● Chargeable premiums   **5.22** £

● Reverse premiums   **5.22A** £

boxes 5.19 + 5.20 + 5.22 + 5.22A
5.23 £

■ *Expenses* (do not include figures you have already put in boxes 5.2 to 5.7 on Page L1)

● Rent, rates, insurance, ground rents etc.   **5.24** £

- Repairs, maintenance and renewals **5.25** £
- Finance charges, including interest **5.26** £
- Legal and professional costs **5.27** £
- Costs of services provided, including wages **5.28** £
- Other expenses **5.29** £

total of boxes 5.24 to 5.29
5.30 £

Net profit (put figures in brackets if a loss)

box 5.23 *minus* box 5.30
5.31 £

■ *Tax adjustments*

- Private use **5.32** £
- Balancing charges **5.33** £

box 5.32 + box 5.33
5.34 £

- Rent a Room exempt amount **5.35** £
- Capital allowances **5.36** £
- Tick box 5.36A if box 5.36 includes a claim for 100% capital allowances for flats over shops **5.36A**
- Tick box 5.36B if box 5.36 includes enhanced capital allowances for environmentally friendly expenditure **5.36B**
- 10% wear and tear **5.37** £
- Furnished holiday lettings losses (from box 5.18) **5.38** £

boxes 5.35 to box 5.38
5.39 £

Adjusted profit (if loss enter '0' in box 5.40 and put the loss in box 5.41)

boxes 5.31 + 5.34 *minus* box 5.39
5.40 £

Adjusted loss (if you have entered '0' in box 5.40)

boxes 5.31 + 5.34 *minus* box 5.39
5.41 £

- Loss brought forward from previous year **5.42** £

Profit for the year

box 5.40 *minus* box 5.42
5.43 £

■ *Losses etc*

- Loss offset against total income (read the note on page LN8) **5.44** £
- Loss to carry forward to following year **5.45** £
- Tick box 5.46 if these Pages include details of property let jointly **5.46**
- Tick box 5.47 if **all** property income ceased in the year to 5 April 2004 **and** you don't expect to receive such income again, in the year to 5 April 2005 **5.47**

What to enter

The relevant income, expenditure and losses. See page 62 for expenditure you can claim and see page 51 for capital allowances details.

Tax tip **Rent-a-room scheme with income over £4,250 a year**
You have the option of either paying tax on the excess over £4,250 without any deduction for allowable expenses, or calculating any total profit made (gross rents less actual allowable expenses) and paying tax on that profit in the normal way. An individual's £4,250 limit is halved if, at any time during a tax year, someone else received income from letting the same property.

What expenses can you claim against property income?

Consider some or all of the following:

- Rent paid, business and water rates.
- General maintenance and repairs of the property, garden, furniture and fittings.
- Costs of agents for letting and collecting rents.
- Insurance.
- Council tax.
- Interest payable on a loan to purchase or improve investment property.
- Charges for preparing inventories.
- Legal fees on renewing a tenancy agreement, for leases of not more than 50 years, or on the initial grant of a lease not exceeding 21 years.
- Accountancy fees to prepare and agree your income.
- Costs of collecting rents, which could in some cases include your travelling expenses to and from the property.

- Costs of services e.g. porters, cleaners, security.
- Wear and tear allowance for furniture and fittings – generally 10 per cent of the basic rent receivable. As an alternative, the cost of renewals may be claimed.

Tax tip Joint ownership

If a husband and wife own a property that is let, the tax office will assume that any income from this asset is divided equally. You should enter in your tax return one half of the income and expenses, and tick box 5.46 to indicate to the tax office that it is a joint holding.

If the ownership is not held equally, then ask your tax office for form 17 in which you can jointly declare the actual ownership split. Such declaration takes effect from the date it is made provided that the form is sent to your tax office within 60 days.

Q6 Foreign income

If you receive savings income, pensions, social security benefits and property income from abroad you will have ticked the 'Yes' box on page 2 of your tax return and you will need to fill in these supplementary pages where applicable.

Foreign savings 6.1A – 6.2

Fill this in if
You receive interest and other income from overseas savings or dividends if you are not assessed on a remittance basis (see also page 64).

Where to find the information
Interest statements and dividend vouchers.

Country A (tick box if income is unremittable ▼)	Amount before tax B	UK tax C	Foreign tax D	Amount chargeable E (tick box to claim foreign tax credit relief ▼)
Interest, and other income from overseas savings - see Notes, page FN4	£	£	£	£
	£	£	£	£
	£	£	£	£
	£	£	£	£
	£	£	£	£
	total of column above **6.1A** £			total of column above **6.1** £
Dividends - see Notes, page FN4	£	£	£	£
	£	£	£	£
	£	£	£	£
	£	£	£	£
	£	£	£	£
	total of column above **6.2A** £			total of column above **6.2** £

What to enter
Each source of income on a separate line. If any savings are in joint names remember to only include your share. Include income from the Channel Islands or Republic of Ireland.

Do not include
Earnings from work done abroad – these go in the Employment, Self Employment or Partnership supplementary pages.

Capital gains on overseas investments go in the Capital Gains supplementary pages.

Tax tip Overseas income
Income from overseas is taxable in the UK even if tax has been deducted, although you can claim foreign tax credit relief in most cases (see page 65).

If you are not domiciled or not ordinarily resident in the UK you will need to fill in the Non-residence supplementary pages (see page 75).

There are many rules and regulations regarding the tax treatment of income from abroad and if you are in any doubt it is wise to consult an accountant or tax adviser.

Other foreign savings, pensions, benefits, etc. 6.3 − 6.8

Fill this in if
You receive interest and dividend income assessed on a remittance basis.

You receive pensions, Social Security benefits and other income from overseas.

Where to find the information
Interest statements, dividend vouchers, pension statements, etc.

Fill in columns A to E, and tick the box in column E to claim foreign tax credit relief.

	Country A (tick box if income is unremittable)	Amount before tax B	UK tax C	Foreign tax D	Amount chargeable E (tick box to claim foreign tax credit relief)
Dividends, interest and other savings income taxable on the remittance basis - see Notes, page FN2		£ / £ / £ / £ / £			£ / £ / £ / £ / £
Pensions - see Notes, page FN5		£ / £ / £	£ / £ / £	£ / £ / £	£ / £ / £
Social security benefits - see Notes, page FN6		£ / £ / £		£ / £ / £	£ / £ / £
Income from land and property IMPORTANT - see Notes, pages FN6 to FN10		£	£	£	£
Chargeable premiums		£	£	£	£
Income received by an overseas trust, company, and other entity (excluding dividends) - see Notes, page FN10		£ / £ / £ / £	£ / £ / £ / £	£ / £ / £ / £	£ / £ / £ / £

total of column above **6.3** £   total of column above **6.4** £

| Dividend income received by an overseas trust, company or other entity - see Notes, page FN10 | | £ / £ / £ | £ / £ / £ | £ / £ / £ | £ / £ / £ |

total of column above **6.3A** £   total of column above **6.4A** £

- Disposals of holdings in offshore funds, income from non-resident trusts and benefits received from overseas trusts, companies and other entities - see Notes, page FN11.   **6.5** £

Tick box 6.5A if you are omitting income from boxes 6.4, 6.4A or 6.5 - see Notes, pages FN11 and FN12.   **6.5A**

- Gains on foreign life insurance policies etc. - see Notes page FN12. Number of years **6.6**   Tax treated as paid **6.7** £   Gains(s) **6.8** £

What to enter
Each source of income on a separate line, making sure you tick the right-hand column if you want to offset any foreign tax deducted against your UK liability.

Tax tip Land and property
Don't fill in the totals for land and property in this section until you have completed boxes 6.11 to 6.38.

Foreign tax credit relief 6.9 – 6.10

Fill this in if
You have had foreign tax deducted from any of your income – including employment income which you will have entered in other sections of the return, or you had foreign tax deducted from any capital gains made from overseas investments.

Use a separate line for each type of income.

Where to find the information
Interest and dividend vouchers, employment records, contract notes for investment sales and purchases.

Foreign tax credit relief for foreign tax paid on employment, self-employment and other income

See Notes, page FN14

Enter in this column the Page number in your Tax Return from which information is taken. Do this for each item for which you are claiming foreign tax credit relief ▼	Country A	Foreign tax D	Amount chargeable E tick box to claim foreign tax credit relief ▼
		£	£
		£	£
		£	£
		£	£
		£	£
		£	£
		£	£

- If you are calculating your tax, enter the total foreign tax credit relief on your income in box 6.9 - *see Notes, pages FN15 and FN16.*   **6.9** £

Foreign tax credit relief for foreign tax paid on chargeable gains reported on your Capital Gains Pages

See Notes, page FN15

Amount of gain under UK rules	Period over which UK gain accrued	Amount of gain under foreign tax rules	Period over which foreign gain accrued	Foreign tax paid D tick box to claim foreign tax credit relief ▼
£	days	£	days	£
£	days	£	days	£
£	days	£	days	£
£	days	£	days	£
£	days	£	days	£
£	days	£	days	£

- If you are calculating your tax, enter the total foreign tax credit relief on your gains in box 6.10 - *see Notes, page FN15.*   **6.10** £

What to enter
The relevant figures under each box. The calculations are very complicated and you will need the Inland Revenue working sheets which should come with your tax return or you can download them from www.inlandrevenue.gov.uk

Income from land and property abroad 6.11 – 6.39

Fill this in if
You receive income from land and property located abroad.

Where to find the information
Your property records and rent receipts. Invoices for expenses.

Address of property

Postcode

- Income - total rents and other receipts (excluding chargeable premiums) **6.11** £
- Tick box 6.11A if box 6.11 contains income from more than one property **6.11A**
- Tick box 6.11B if the income in box 6.11 is unremittable. **6.11B**

Expenses - see Notes, page FN7

- Rent, rates, insurance, etc **6.12** £
- Repairs, maintenance and renewals **6.13** £
- Finance charges, including interest **6.14** £
- Legal and professional costs **6.15** £
- Costs of services provided **6.16** £
- Other expenses **6.17** £ | total boxes 6.12 to 6.17 **6.18** £

Net profit (or loss) - enter loss in brackets | box 6.11 *minus* 6.18 **6.19** £

Tax adjustments - see Notes, page FN9

- Private use proportions **6.20** £
- Balancing charges **6.21** £ | box 6.20 + box 6.21 **6.22** £

- Capital allowances **6.23** £
- Tick box 6.23A if box 6.23 includes enhanced capital allowances for environmentally friendly expenditure **6.23A**
- 10% wear and tear **6.24** £ | box 6.23 + box 6.24 **6.25** £

Adjusted profit (if loss, enter '0' here, and enter loss in box 6.27) | box 6.19 + box 6.22 minus box 6.25 **6.26** £

Adjusted loss (if you have entered '0' in box 6.26) | box 6.19 + box 6.22 minus box 6.25 **6.27** £

> Fill in boxes 6.28 to 6.32 (if you have completed only one Page F4) **or** boxes 6.33 to 6.38 if you have completed a separate Page F4 for each property.

- Taxable profit or allowable loss from box 6.26 or 6.27 (enter a loss in brackets) **6.28** £

minus losses brought forward from earlier years **6.29** £

box 6.28 minus 6.29

Total taxable profits (if box 6.28 is a profit and is more than box 6.29) **6.30** £

Copy to column B on Page F2

or loss to carry forward (if box 6.28 is a profit but less than box 6.29, enter box 6.29 *minus* box 6.28, or, if box 6.28 is a loss, enter box 6.28 *plus* box 6.29) **6.31** £

- If you have only one property or your properties are all in the same foreign country and foreign tax was deducted, enter the tax paid **6.32** £

Copy to column D on Page F2 and fill in columns A and E as appropriate

*If you have filled in more than one Page F4 enter details below using a separate line for each overseas let property. **Exclude** any unremittable income from the 'Taxable profit or loss' column.*

Country	Taxable profit or loss (from box 6.26 or 6.27)	Foreign tax	Amount chargeable
1	£	£	£
2	£	£	£
3	£	£	£
4	£	£	£
5	£	£	£
6	£	£	£

total column above
6.33 £

minus losses brought forward from earlier years **6.34** £

Total taxable profits **6.35** £ **6.36** £ **6.37** £

Copy to column B on Page F2 *Copy to column D on Page F2* *Copy to column E on Page F2*

or loss to carry forward **6.38** £

6.39 *Additional information*

What to enter

Details of income and your expenses claim. You will need a separate sheet for each property.

Q7 Trusts, settlements and estates

If you have income from trusts, settlements or estates, then you will have ticked the 'Yes' box on page 2 of your tax return and will need to fill in these supplementary pages where applicable.

Income from trusts and settlements, summary of tax rates 7.1 – 7.12A

Fill this in if
You have received income from trusts or settlements.

Where to find the information
Form 185, which the trustees or personal representative will have given you, will show the net amount and the rate of tax credit applicable. This rate will vary depending on the type of trust and the type of income.

■ *Income taxed at:*

	Income receivable	Tax paid	Taxable amount
● the 'rate applicable to trusts'	7.1 £	7.2 £	7.3 £
● the basic rate	7.4 £	7.5 £	7.6 £
● the lower rate	7.7 £	7.8 £	7.9 £
● the dividend rate	7.10 £	7.11 £	7.12 £

Tick this box if you have included in your Tax Return, income from trusts or settlements whose trustees are not resident in the UK for tax purposes 7.12A ☐

What to enter
The relevant net income, the tax credits and the gross amounts by adding the two figures together.

Use the working sheets at the end of this book if you have several types of income.

Special rules also apply to certain types of income from Interest in Possession Trusts.

If you are unsure of the rules, consult the notes on trusts accompanying your tax return or request helpsheet IR270.

Do not include
Income from a 'bare trust'. You are considered to be in control of such assets and the income from them and you need to enter such income in the main tax return and relevant supplementary sheets.

Income from foreign trusts should be declared in the Foreign supplementary pages.

Income from estates of deceased persons 7.13 – 7.31

Fill this in if

You have received income as a beneficiary from an estate during the period it is being wound up by the executors, etc..

Where to find the information

A tax certificate R185 will have been given to you by the executors, etc., which should give you all the details you require.

■ *Income bearing:*

	Income receivable	Tax paid	Taxable amount
● basic rate tax	7.13 £	7.14 £	7.15 £
● lower rate tax	7.16 £	7.17 £	7.18 £
● repayable dividend rate	7.19 £	7.20 £	7.21 £
● non-repayable basic rate tax	7.22 £	7.23 £	7.24 £
● non-repayable lower rate tax	7.25 £	7.26 £	7.27 £
● non-repayable dividend rate	7.28 £	7.29 £	7.30 £
● total foreign tax for which tax credit relief not claimed		7.31 £	

What to enter

The relevant income received, tax deducted and gross amount, split between the various rates. Form R185 will state whether the rate is repayable or non-repayable.

Q8 Capital gains

If you have made a capital gain or loss when you have sold an asset, given away or transferred an asset or received compensation for an asset or possession then you will have ticked one of the 'Yes' boxes on page 2 of your tax return and you will need to fill in these supplementary pages where applicable.

Quoted shares/unit trusts, etc. Page CG1

Fill this in if
You have sold, transferred or given away any quoted shares, including unit trusts and shares in an open-ended investment company (oeic).

(If your share transactions are relatively straightforward and no other assets are involved then this is the only section of this supplementary return that you need to complete.)

Where to find the information
Contract notes or correspondence regarding the relevant shares.

Total gains	**F1** £		Total your gains in column E and enter the amount in box F1
Total losses	**F2** £		Total your losses in column E and enter the amount in box F2
Net gain/(loss)	**F3** £	box F1 *minus* box F2	If your net gains are not more than £7,900 **or** you have a net loss, there is no liability. If you have a net loss, please fill in the losses summary on Page CG8 otherwise carry on to box F4
minus income losses set against gains	**F4** £		
	F5 £	box F3 *minus* box F4	If your gains are now £7,900 or below, there is no liability; copy box F5 to box F7 and complete Page CG8. Otherwise, carry on to box F6
minus losses brought forward	**F6** £		Enter losses brought forward up to the **smaller** of either the total losses brought forward or the figure in box F5 **minus** £7,900
Total taxable gains	**F7** £	box F5 *minus* box F6	Copy this figure to box 8.7 on Page CG8 (if F7 is blank because there is no liability, leave 8.7 blank).

What to enter
Disposal details of each of the relevant shares. Boxes F1 to F7 are summary boxes – carefully follow the wording and instructions on the right hand side.

Tax tip Indexation allowance
An indexation allowance can be claimed for assets held prior to 30 April 1998. The notes accompanying these supplementary pages will show a table giving the relevant percentages.

Do not include
Any shares etc., that you held at 31 March 1982 or any shares, etc. on which you want to claim taper relief or other tax relief (like EIS relief) – for these you will need to fill in other boxes (see opposite).

Disposals of other assets Pages CG2 – CG7

Fill this in if
You have made disposals of unquoted shares, or quoted shares on which you are claiming taper relief or other relief (including indexation) or quoted shares you held prior to 31 March 1982.

You have made disposals of land, buildings or unquoted shares.

Where to find the information
Correspondence and invoices or contract notes covering the purchase and sale (or upkeep) of any of the relevant assets.

You may also need some evidence of an asset's valuation at 31 March 1982.

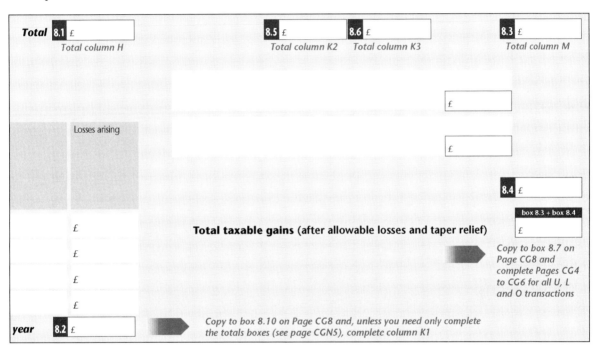

What to enter
Prior to the boxes 8.1 – 8.4 reproduced above there are endless columns for the various types of assets and you need to work through the sequences including using the abbreviation letters (Q, U, L, T and O) for ease of identification.

Do not include
Any assets that are exempt from capital gains tax (see table on page 72).

Tax tip Professional advice
The capital gains system is very complex, with myriad rules and regulations. It is wise to obtain professional advice if your capital gains affairs are not straightforward.

Table of capital gains tapering relief

Gains on business assets			Gains on non-business assets		
Number of complete years after 5 April 1998 for which asset held	Percentage of gain chargeable	Equivalent tax rates for higher-rate taxpayer	Number of complete years after 5 April 1998 for which asset held	Percentage of gain chargeable	Equivalent tax rates for higher-rate /20 per cent rate taxpayer★
0	100 (100)	40 (40)	0	100	40 / 20
1	50 (87.5)	20 (35)	1	100	40 / 20
2	25 (75)	10 (30)	2	100	40 / 20
3	25 (50)	10 (20)	3	95	38 / 19
4	25 (25)	10 (10)	4	90	36 / 18
5	25 (25)	10 (10)	5	85	34 / 17
6	25 (25)	10 (10)	6	80	32 / 16
7	25 (25)	10 (10)	7	75	30 / 15
8	25 (25)	10 (10)	8	70	28 / 14
9	25 (25)	10 (10)	9	65	26 / 13
10 or more	25 (25)	10 (10)	10 or more	60	24 / 12

Notes
★ Since 6 April 2000, gains may also be charged at the 10 per cent starting rate, depending on your total income.

Assets that are free from capital gains tax

Private motor cars.

A house owned and occupied by you which is your main residence.

Chattels – such as jewellery, pictures and. furniture – where the proceeds are £6,000 or less, with marginal relief up to £15,000.

Life policies and deferred annuities (unless sold on by the original owner).

National Savings Certificates.

Shares subscribed for under the BES and EIS.

Shares subscribed for in approved quoted Venture Capital Trusts.

Personal Equity Plan (PEP) investments.

Individual Savings Accounts (ISAs).

Save As You Earn schemes.

TESSA accounts.

Government stocks and public corporation stocks guaranteed by the Government.

Qualifying corporate bonds.

Gambling, pools and lottery winnings and prizes.

Decorations for gallantry, unless purchased.

Compensation for damages.

Gifts of assets to a charity and certain sports clubs.

Gifts of outstanding public interest given to the nation.

Land and buildings given to the National Trust.

Compensation for mis-sold personal pensions and AVCs between 29–4–88 and 30–6–94.

Foreign currency for personal use.

Gains and losses summary Page CG8

Fill this in if
You have completed any of the boxes so far in these supplementary pages.

Where to find the information
From the entries you have made in previous pages or from your own records of losses brought forward from previous years.

Once you have completed Page CG1, or Pages CG2 to CG6, fill in this Page.

Have you 'ticked' any row in Column B, 'Tick box if estimate or valuation used' on Pages CG1 or CG2 or in Column C on Page CG2 'Tick box if asset held at 31 March 1982'?   **YES** ☐

Have you given details in Column G on Pages CG2 and CG3 of any Capital Gains reliefs claimed or due?   **YES** ☐

Are you claiming, and/or using, any clogged losses (see Notes, page CGN11)?   **YES** ☐

Enter from Page CG1 or column AA on Page CG2:

- the number of transactions in quoted shares or other securities   **box Q** ☐

- the number of transactions in other shares or securities   **box U** ☐

- the number of transactions in land and property   **box L** ☐

- the number of gains attributed to settlor   **box T** ☐

- the number of other transactions   **box O** ☐

Total taxable gains (from Page CG1 or Page CG3)   **8.7** £

Your taxable gains *minus* the annual exempt amount of £7,900 (leave blank if '0' or negative)   box 8.7 *minus* £7,900   **8.8** £

Additional liability in respect of non-resident or dual resident trusts (see Notes, page CGN7)   **8.9** £

Capital losses

(If your loss arose on a transaction with a connected person, see page CGN14, you can only set that loss against gains you make on disposals to that same connected person. See the notes on clogged losses on page CGN11.)

■ This year's losses

- Total (normally from box 8.2 on Page CG3 or box F2 on Page CG1. But, if you have clogged losses, see Notes, page CGN11)   **8.10** £

- Used against gains (total of column K1 on Page CG3, or the smaller of boxes F1 and F2 on Page CG1)   **8.11** £

- Used against earlier years' gains (generally only available to personal representatives, see Notes, page CGN11)   **8.12** £

- Used against income (only losses of the type described on page CGN9 can be used against income)   **8.13A** £   amount claimed against income of 2003-04
  8.13B £   amount claimed against income of 2002-03   box 8.13A + box 8.13B   **8.13** £

- This year's unused losses   box 8.10 *minus* (boxes 8.11 + 8.12 + 8.13)   **8.14** £

■ Summary of earlier years' losses

- Unused losses of 1996-97 and later years   **8.15** £

- Used this year (losses from box 8.15 are used in priority to losses from box 8.18) (column K3 on Page CG3 or box F6 on Page CG1)   **8.16** £

- Remaining unused losses of 1996-97 and later years   box 8.15 *minus* box 8.16   **8.17** £

• Unused losses of 1995-96 and earlier years	**8.18**	£
• Used this year (losses from box 8.15 are used in priority to losses from box 8.18) (column K3 on Page CG3 or box F6 on Page CG1)	**8.19** box 8.6 *minus* box 8.16 (or box F6 *minus* box 8.16)	£
■ *Total of unused losses to carry forward*		
• Carried forward losses of 1996-97 and later years	**8.20** box 8.14 + box 8.17	£
• Carried forward losses of 1995-96 and earlier years	**8.21** box 8.18 *minus* box 8.19	£

What to enter

Answer the first three questions then fill in boxes Q to O and 8.7 to 8.9. These are summary boxes of the information you have already supplied.

Boxes 8.10 to 8.21 represent a summary of the various types of losses that you can use against a capital gain, or losses brought forward or carried forward.

Tax tip Married couple's allowance
Married couples are each entitled to their own tax-free allowance for capital gains tax but if it is not used each year then it is lost. Consider transferring some assets between partners to make better use of the exemption limits.

Tax tip Venture capital trust
If you have made a large capital gain which will result in a large tax bill, then consider taking advantage of the generous tax breaks offered by investing in a venture capital trust or enterprise investment scheme (see page 22).

Q9 Non-residence, etc.

If you want to claim non-residence (or non-domicile) status for this tax year you will have ticked 'Yes' on page 2 of your tax return and you will need to fill in these supplementary pages where applicable.

Non-residence, etc. 9.1 – 9.35

Fill this in if
You know that you are non-resident or not domiciled in the UK for tax purposes, or if you have moved abroad or have been living abroad, for this may affect your tax status and tax liabilities (only the first part of the form is reproduced here).

Where to find the information
Your own records from overseas employment remuneration and letters from current or previous employers and possibly UK and overseas tax authorities.

Residence status

I am *(please tick appropriate box)*

• resident in the UK	9.1	
• ordinarily resident in the UK	9.3	
• not domiciled in the UK (and it is relevant to my Income Tax or Capital Gains Tax liability)	9.5	
• claiming personal allowances as a non-resident	9.7	

• not resident in the UK	9.2	
• not ordinarily resident in the UK	9.4	
• claiming split-year treatment	9.6	
• resident in a country other than the UK (under a double taxation agreement) at the same time as being resident in the UK	9.8	

What to enter
These supplementary pages (up to box 9.35) contain a sequence of questions so that the tax office can establish your status for tax purposes.

Tax tip Tax status and liability
If you work or live abroad, the number and frequency of visits to the UK in any one tax year can affect your UK tax liability and it is important to keep a record of the dates of your visits.

The rules governing the legal status of a person and the tax implications are amongst some of the most difficult tax legislation, and it is wise to get a tax adviser to handle these matters for you.

PAYE coding notice

The tax office gives employers a PAYE code for each of their employees so that they know how much of your pay is to be tax free. Your employer is told only the code (not the full details) so they cannot check whether or not it is correct. The code is made up from the information your tax office has on their files, either as a result of information that they have found out or from a tax return sent in by you. The tax office send you a coding notice similar to that shown below, which you need to check. Help on how to do this is given on the next page.

Inland Revenue

PAYE Coding Notice

Tax code for tax year

P2

Please keep all your coding notices. You may need to refer to them if you have to fill in a tax return. Please also quote your tax reference and National Insurance number if you contact us.

Issued by

Tax reference	National Insurance number

Your tax code for the year shown above is

This tax code is used to deduct tax payable on your income from

_____

_____

If you move to another job, your new employer will normally continue to use this tax code. The tax code is worked out as follows:

The '**See note**' columns below refer to the numbered notes in the leaflet '**Understanding Your Tax Code**'. This tells you about the **letter part** of your tax code.

Check that your details are correct. If you think they're wrong, or you have any questions, ask me (my details are above).

This coding notice replaces any previous notice for the year.

See note	Your tax allowances	£	See note	Amounts taken away from your total allowances	£
A	**Total allowances**		**B**	**Total deductions**	

C	Your tax free amount for the year is £	, making your tax code	see example overleaf

How your PAYE code is calculated

Left-hand boxes

In the left-hand boxes of your coding notice will be shown your allowances and allowable expenses, etc.

If you are a higher-rate taxpayer then any allowable payments on which only basic rate tax has been deducted (e.g. personal pension payments, charity gift relief, retirement annuity relief) will be shown here.

If you or your wife were born before 6 April 1935 you will get a higher personal allowance, but this may be restricted depending on your income level (see page 97); *any restriction will be shown on the right-hand side.* Similarly, if you are entitled to the Married Couple's allowance.

Any transfer of allowances will also be listed here (see page 29).

Right-hand boxes

The right-hand side boxes of your coding notice will show any taxable State pension or benefits you are likely to receive and any company benefits, e.g. company car, private fuel, medical insurance.

Other figures might refer to property income or casual earnings declared by you on your tax return (or an estimate made by the tax office).

Any untaxed interest will be stated here. Any under- or over-payment of tax will refer to a previous year.

You only get relief at 10 per cent for the married couple's allowance, so a restriction (or claw back) adjustment will be shown here.

Your code is found by deducting the total of the right-hand side (B) from the left-hand side (A); the last figure is omitted and a letter added. The higher your code, the lower your tax, unless you have a K prefix code.

What do the letters mean?

The letter shown after your code defines your status. For example, L = basic personal allowance; P = full personal allowance if aged 65–74 with V being used if you are also entitled to the married couple's allowance and you are on basic rate tax; Y = personal allowance for those aged 75 or over.

OT means that no allowances have been given – that is often used if you haven't sent in a tax return for a long time or your tax affairs are very complicated. Other codes (BR, DO, T and NT) are sometimes used if you are working for more than one employer or have complicated tax affairs.

Sometimes your taxable benefits will exceed your allowances – for example, if you are taxed on car and fuel benefits and private health benefits, or owe back tax. In these cases a K code is used so that your employer can recoup this tax on behalf of the tax office.

> **Tax tip** Coding notice
> It is important to check your tax code as a mistake could lead to a large underpayment accumulating and, in recent year, there have been a number of problems with the coding of car benefits. You can go back up to six years to claim any overpayment of tax.
>
> If your coding notice is wrong, write to the tax office, or if you haven't filled in a tax return for a year or two, then ask for a tax return and fill it in.

Tax repayments

At the end of each tax year you should check to see exactly what income you received during the year and what tax you have actually paid. Use the Quick Tax Check on page 91.

If you have paid too much you can get a repayment of tax. To reclaim tax ask your tax office for form R40. Complete it in the same way as a tax return and send the form to your tax office. You will also find leaflet IR110 very informative.

The forms are available from your tax office by telephoning 0845 9000 404 and there is a taxback helpline for savers who need to claim a tax repayment – it is 0845 077 6543.

Where most of your income has already had tax deducted before you receive it, you may be able to make quarterly, half-yearly or annual repayment claims.

Is tax being deducted from your savings?

If your total income from all sources for the year does not exceed your allowances and you have any interest from banks, building societies or local authorities, you should register to have such interest paid to you without tax being deducted.

Ask your bank, building society or local authority for form R85, complete it and return it to the branch that holds your account; ask any tax office for booklet IR110 – this has lots of helpful advice and includes form R85 – or call the Inland Revenue registration helpline on 0845 980 0645.

 **Inland Revenue**

Savings: application to receive interest without tax taken off

Please read the notes on the back of this form. Then, if you can receive interest without tax taken off, complete the form and return it to your bank, building society, or local authority. They will arrange for your interest to be paid without tax taken off. As they will not acknowledge receipt of the form, you may wish to take a copy for your records.

Joint accounts - each saver must check to see if they can receive their share of the interest without tax taken off and if so complete their own form.

This form is available in a large print version.

Name of bank, building society or local authority	
Branch	

Account number(s)		Is this a joint account?	Yes	No
			☐	☐
			☐	☐

Details of employee leaving work (form P45)

When you leave an employment, your employer must give you a P45 form. You will get three parts:

Part 1A you keep yourself as a record of your earnings and tax paid, etc.

Parts 2 and 3 you give to your new employer if you start another job. Your new employer will keep part 2, and will complete part 3 and send it to their tax office so that your tax file can be kept up to date and the tax inspector is aware of your movements.

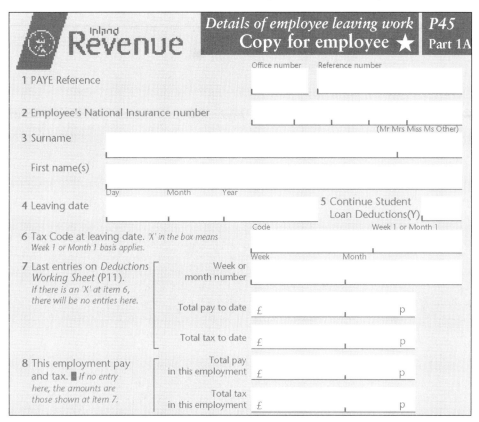

What to do with this form if you have ceased work permanently

Send the form to your tax office whose district is stamped on the form. Also write a letter confirming that you have either retired, ceased working or have become self-employed and ask for a claim form for any tax repayment due.

What to do with this form if you have ceased work temporarily

When you change employment or are made redundant, and there is a gap between one job and the next, send in your form P45 as above, stating that you are temporarily unemployed. Alternatively, if you are claiming the jobseeker's allowance, hand your P45 to your benefit office and they will advise you on the proportion of any benefit that is taxable. Normally any adjustments to your tax liability will be made when you start a new employment in the current tax year.

If you do not start a job by the following 5 April, check your total income and tax to see if there is a repayment or underpayment of tax due (use the quick guide on page 91).

Certificate of pay, income tax and NIC (form P60)

Your employer has by law to give you a P60 form by 31 May after the end of every tax year.

It may have slight variations in design, but it has to contain the following information:

Do not destroy

For employer's use

Employee's details

Sex

National Insurance number

"M" if Ma
"F" if Fem

Surname

First two forenames

Works/payroll no. etc

National Insurance contributions in this employment (Note: LEL = Lower Earnings Limit, U

NIC table letter	Earnings at the LEL (where earnings are equal to or exceed the LEL) (whole £s only)	Earnings above the LEL, up to and including the Earnings Threshold (whole £s only)	Earnings above the Earnings Threshold, up to and including the UEL (whole £s only)	
	1a £	1b £	1c £	
				Employee's up to and

1f £   p

Box 1f applies only to employees in contracted-out occupational pension schemes

Certificate by Employer/Paying Office:
This form shows your total pay for Income Tax purposes in this employment for the year. Any overtime, bonus, commission etc, statutory sick pay or statutory maternity pay is included. It also shows, for this employment, total Income Tax and National Insurance contributions deducted (less any refunds), Student Loan deductions made, and Tax Credits paid to you.

BS 6/02

Pay and Income Tax details

Pay

In previous employment(s)

In this employment ★

Total for year

Employee's Widows & Orphans/Life Assurance contributions in this employment

Your National Insurance number.

The amounts paid by you and your employer in National Insurance contributions.

These boxes will have totals for the pay you have received from the employer who has issued you with this form together with the amount of tax deducted. There will also be totals for pay and tax in respect of previous employers for whom you worked in this tax year.

Indicates a deduction for this insurance.

Tax tip What to do with your P60 form
Keep it as a record of your earnings for the tax year and the amount of tax deducted.
Use it to fill in your tax return.
Use it as additional proof of income if you arrange a mortgage or loan.
Use it to check any tax assessment that is sent to you.

Tax tip Pension forecasts
Write to the DWP at State Pension Forecasting Team, The Pension Service, Room TB001, Tyneview Park, Whitley Road, Newcastle upon Tyne NE98 1BA if you want a written State retirement pension projection.
You can also check that you have made sufficient contributions to qualify for the maximum State pension and other benefits.

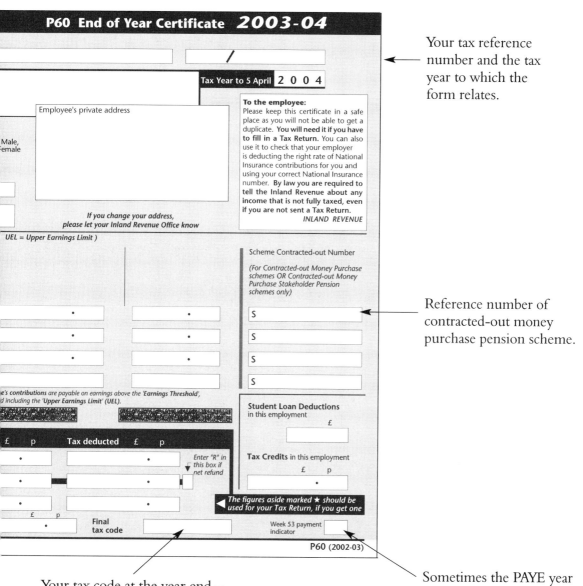

Your tax reference number and the tax year to which the form relates.

Reference number of contracted-out money purchase pension scheme.

Your tax code at the year end – this will probably also apply for 2004–2005, so check to see that it is correct (see page 77).

Sometimes the PAYE year has 53 weeks instead of 52. (This box is for the convenience of the tax office.)

Return of expenses and benefits (form P11D)

The form reproduced below has to be completed annually by an employer for all staff who receive earnings, expenses and potential benefits which total £8,500 a year or more, and for most directors. There is a legal obligation for all employers to complete and return this form to the Inland Revenue and to give each employee a copy of the form by 6 July after each tax year.

You will need the figures that have been declared on the P11D form to enter in the Employment supplementary pages of your tax return (see page 39) – and if you haven't filled in a tax return then you should find these figures on your PAYE coding notice, which you should check (see page 77). If you have changed jobs during the year, your employer will probably have not given you a P11D form for the period you were employed as the forms are not usually completed until the end of the

tax year. You should write to your ex-employer asking for a copy if you don't get one by 6 July.

Sometimes an employer gets a dispensation, or has a PAYE settlement agreement with the Inland Revenue and doesn't have to include certain routine expenses or benefits on a P11D form (e.g. reimbursed travelling and subsistence expenses at an approved rate); in these cases you do not have to declare the expenditure and you will not be taxed on it.

The boxes with 1A on the right hand side identify those benefits on which the employer (but not the employee) has to pay Class 1A National Insurance contributions.

You may be liable to Class 1 National Insurance contributions on certain expenses and benefits provided by your employer and this liability will be collected via your payroll deductions.

Inland Revenue — **P11D EXPENSES AND BENEFITS 2003-04**

Note to employer
Complete this return for a director, or an employee who earned at a rate of £8,500 a year or more during the year 6 April 2003 to 5 April 2004. Do not include expenses and benefits covered by a dispensation or PAYE settlement agreement. Read the P11D Guide and Booklet 480, Chapter 24, before you complete the form. You must give a copy of this information to the director or employee by 6 July 2004. The term employee is used to cover both directors and employees throughout the rest of this form. **Send the completed P11D and form P11D(b) to the Inland Revenue office by 6 July 2004.**

Note to employee
Your employer has filled in this form. Keep it in a safe place as you may not be able to get a duplicate. You will need it for your tax records and to complete your 2003-04 Tax Return if you get one. Your tax code may need to be adjusted to take account of the information given on this P11D. The box numbers on this P11D have the same numbering as the Employment Pages of the Tax Return, for example, 1.12. Include the total figures in the corresponding box on the Tax Return, unless you think some other figure is more appropriate.

Employer's details
Employer's name

PAYE tax reference

Employee's details
Employee's name

If a director tick here ▶

Works number /department

National Insurance number

Employers pay Class 1A National Insurance contributions on most benefits. These are shown in boxes which are brown and have a **1A** indicator

A | **Assets transferred (cars, property, goods or other assets)** | Cost/ Market value | Amount made good or from which tax deducted | Cash equivalent |
Description of asset | £ | – £ | = **1.12** £ | **1A**

B | **Payments made on behalf of employee** | | | |
Description of payment | | | **1.12** £ |
Tax on notional payments not borne by employee within 30 days of receipt of each notional payment | | | **1.12** £ |

C | **Vouchers or credit cards** | Gross amount | Amount made good or from which tax deducted | Cash equivalent |
Value of vouchers and payments made using credit cards or tokens | £ | – £ | = **1.13** £ |

D | **Living accommodation** | | | Cash equivalent |
Cash equivalent of accommodation provided for employee, or his/ her family or household | | | **1.14** £ | **1A**

E | **Mileage allowance and passenger payments** | | | Taxable amount |
Amount of car and mileage allowances paid for employee's own vehicle, and passenger payments, in excess of maximum exempt amounts (See P11D Guide for 2003-04 exempt rates) | | | **1.15** £ |

F **Cars and car fuel** *If more than two cars were made available, either at the same time or in succession, please give details on a separate sheet*

	Car 1	Car 2
Make and Model		
Date first registered	/ /	/ /
Approved CO2 emissions figure for cars registered on or after 1 January 1998 *Tick box if the car does not have an approved CO2 figure*	g/km □ *See P11D Guide for details of cars that have no approved CO2 figure*	g/km □ *See P11D Guide for details of cars that have no approved CO2 figure*
Engine size	cc	cc
Type of fuel or power used *Please use the key letter shown in the P11D Guide (2004)*		
Dates car was available *Only enter a 'from' or 'to' date if the car was first made available and/or ceased to be available in 2003-04*	From / / to / /	From / / to / /
List price of car *Including car and standard accessories only: if there is no list price, or if it is a classic car, employers see booklet 480; employees see leaflet IR172*	£	£
Accessories *All non-standard accessories, see P11D Guide*	£	£
Capital contributions (maximum £5,000) the employee made towards the cost of car or accessories	£	£
Amount paid by employee for private use of the car	£	£
Cash equivalent of each car	£	£
Total cash equivalent of all cars available in 2003-04		1.16 £ 1A
Cash equivalent of fuel for each car	£	£
Date free fuel was withdrawn (applies to all cars) *Tick if reinstated in year (see P11D Guide)*	/ / □	
Total cash equivalent of fuel for all cars available in 2003-04		1.17 £ 1A

Car benefit

If you are provided with a company car the benefit is calculated as a percentage of the list price of the car (not the amount you paid for it or its secondhand value) and the percentage used depends on the CO_2 emission rating of the vehicle. Any personal contribution of up to £5,000 towards the cost of the car can be deducted from the list price.

Table of car benefits

CO_2 emissions 2003–04	2004–05	Benefit %	CO_2 emissions 2003–04	2004–05	Benefit %	CO_2 emissions 2003–04	2004–05	Benefit %
155	145	15★	195	185	23★	235	225	31★
160	150	16★	200	190	24★	240	230	32★
165	155	17★	205	195	25★	245	235	33★★
170	160	18★	210	200	26★	250	240	34★★★
175	165	19★	215	205	27★	255	245	35†
180	170	20★	220	210	28★			
185	175	21★	225	215	29★	Discounts are available for cars which run on alternative fuel		
190	180	22★	230	220	30★			

For cars with no approved CO_2 emission rating, the benefit percentage will be based on the engine capacity as follows: 0–1400 c.c. 15%★ (15%), 1401–2000 c.c. 25%★ (22%), over 2000 c.c. 35%† (32%) – figures in brackets refer to pre-1988 car registrations.

Notes
Diesel supplements if car runs solely on diesel (waived if Euro 4 diesels): ★Add 3 per cent, ★★add 2 per cent, ★★★add 1 per cent, †maximum charge so no diesel supplement. Also including rotary-engined petrol cars which have no cylinder capacity.

Fuel benefit

If your employer provides fuel for your private motoring and you do not reimburse the full cost, you will be taxed on the benefit. From 6 April 2003 a standard figure of £14,400 is used by the Inland Revenue and the tax benefit will be based on the CO_2 rating percentage of your vehicle (see page 83). Prior to this date, fuel benefit was taxed on the basis of the cc rating of the vehicle.

Mileage allowance

If employers pay a mileage allowance to employees to use their own car or bike for business, then any payment in excess of the official tax-free mileage rates will be liable to tax and National Insurance. The tax-free allowance from 6 April 2003 for cars has been 40p a mile on the first 10,000 business miles in a tax year and 25p a mile thereafter. Any payment over these figures is taxable. An extra 5p a mile can be claimed if you have a business passenger. Allowances for bicycles are 20p a mile and 24p a mile for motor cycles.

G Vans

Cash equivalent of all vans made available for private use — **1.18** £ ___ 1A

H Interest-free and low interest loans

If the total amount outstanding on all loans does not exceed £5,000 at any time in the year, there is no need for details in this section.

	Loan 1	Loan 2
Number of joint borrowers (if applicable)		
Amount outstanding at 5 April 2003 or at date loan was made if later	£	£
Amount outstanding at 5 April 2004 or at date loan was discharged if earlier	£	£
Maximum amount outstanding at any time in the year	£	£
Total amount of interest paid by the borrower in 2003-04– enter "NIL" if none was paid	£	£
Date loan was made in 2003-04 if applicable	/ /	/ /
Date loan was discharged in 2003-04 if applicable	/ /	/ /
Cash equivalent of loans after deducting any interest paid by the borrower	**1.19** £ ___ 1A	**1.19** £ ___ 1A

I Private medical treatment or insurance

	Cost to you	Amount made good or from which tax deducted	Cash equivalent
Private medical treatment or insurance	£	– £	= **1.21** £ ___ 1A

J Qualifying relocation expenses payments and benefits

Non-qualifying benefits and expenses go in N and O below

Excess over £8,000 of all qualifying relocation expenses payments and benefits for each move — **1.22** £ ___ 1A

K Services supplied

	Cost to you	Amount made good or from which tax deducted	Cash equivalent
Services supplied to the employee	£	– £	= **1.22** £ ___ 1A

L Assets placed at the employee's disposal

	Annual value plus expenses incurred	Amount made good or from which tax deducted	Cash equivalent
Description of asset ___	£	– £	= **1.22** £ ___ 1A

M Shares

Tick the box if during the year there have been share-related benefits for the employee ☐

N **Other items (including subscriptions and professional fees)**

		Cost to you	Amount made good or from which tax deducted	Cash equivalent

Description of other items   [_____]   £ [_____] – £ [_____] = **1.22** £ [_____] 1A

Description of other items   [_____]   £ [_____] – £ [_____] = **1.22** £ [_____]

Tax paid

Income tax paid but not deducted from director's remuneration   **1.22** £ [_____]

O **Expenses payments made to, or on behalf of, the employee**

		Cost to you	Amount made good or from which tax deducted	Taxable payment

Travelling and subsistence payments (except mileage allowance payments for employee's own car - *see box E*)   £ [_____] – £ [_____] = **1.23** £ [_____]

Entertainment *(trading organisations read P11D Guide and then enter a tick or a cross as appropriate here)* [ ]   £ [_____] – £ [_____] = **1.23** £ [_____]

General expenses allowance for business travel   £ [_____] – £ [_____] = **1.23** £ [_____]

Payments for use of home telephone   £ [_____] – £ [_____] = **1.23** £ [_____]

Non-qualifying relocation expenses *(those not shown in sections J or N)*   £ [_____] – £ [_____] = **1.23** £ [_____]

Description of other expenses [_____]   £ [_____] – £ [_____] = **1.23** £ [_____]

Is your benefit taxable?

Benefit for 2003–2004	Employees earning £8,500 a year or more and directors	Employees earning less than £8,500 a year
Assets proviced for your use free of charge (e.g. video)	Taxable at 20 per cent of initial market value	Usually tax frcc
Canteen facilities available to directors and staff	Not taxable	Not taxable
Car and bike parking facilities at work	Not taxable	Not taxable
Cash vouchers	Taxable	Taxable
Christmas parties, etc.	Not taxable up to £150 per person in total per year	
Clothing and other goods give to you by your employer	Taxable	Taxable on second-hand value
Company cars, vans, etc.	Taxable at varying rates	Not taxable
Computer equipment provided on loan	Not taxable up to a benefit of £500	Not taxable
Credit cards (for personal, not business expenditure)	Taxable	Taxable
Exam prizes	Not taxable if reasonable and not part of employment contract	
Fuel for private use	Taxable (at scale rate for company cars)	Not taxable
Holidays	Taxable, apart from business element	If employer pays directly, tax free
Interest-free loan	Normally taxable	Not taxable
In-house benefits	Taxable only on the value of the marginal or additional cost to the employer	
Jobfinder's grant	Not taxable	Not taxable
Living accommodation	Normally taxable at annual value unless essential for your employment	
Luncheon vouchers	Tax free up to 15p per working day	
Mileage allowances	Not taxable up to the authorised rates – any excess is taxable	
Mobile telephones provided by employer	Not taxable	Not taxable

Benefit for 2003–2004	Employees earning £8,500 a year or more and directors	Employees earning less than £8,500 a year
Nurseries and play schemes run by employer	Not taxable if on employer's premises or if elsewhere they must be financed and arranged by employer	
Outplacement counselling	Not taxable	Not taxable
Pension contributions and death benefits	Normally tax free	
Private health schemes	Taxable	Not taxable
Prizes and incentive awards	Taxable	Taxable
Relocation expenses (if qualifying)	Tax free up to £8,000	
Retraining and counselling on leaving employment	Not taxable if you have been employed for at least two years	
Scholarships provided by employer's trust	Taxable	Not taxable
Season tickets for travel paid directly by employer	Taxable	Taxable
Share incentive schemes approved by tax inspector	Not taxable	Not taxable
Sick pay schemes	Taxable	Taxable
Workplace sports facilities	Not taxable	Not taxable

How to calculate your own tax

The tax system in the UK is unnecessarily complicated and gets worse year by year as the annual budget statements pile on even more regulations, new types of taxes and tax credits, and endless tinkering with allowances which you can (or cannot) claim.

Do I have to calculate my own tax?
No, you do not have to calculate your own tax at all if you do not want to, but if you do not, how will you ever know if you are paying the correct amount of tax? How will you know if your PAYE code number is correct? How will you know if you should be paying some tax on account during the year or, indeed, claiming a refund?

What do I say to the tax office?
When you complete your tax return, Q18 (see page 30 in this book) asks whether you want to calculate your own tax. If you say 'No' and you send your tax return in before 30 September – or two months after the date the return form was sent to you, if later – the tax office will do it for you. If you send in your return after that date, the tax office will still calculate any tax due (or overpaid), but they will not guarantee to do it before 31 January and if you haven't paid enough you will have to pay interest on the balance due.

If you tick the 'Yes' box in Q18 then you can, if you want to, use the Tax Calculation Guide (SA151W) that will have been sent to you with your tax return.

I don't have a copy of this guide
If the Tax Calculation Guide does not come with your tax return, telephone 0845 9000 404 – this is the Inland Revenue order line – and they will send you a copy and any other form you may request.

What do all the box numbers mean?
All the boxes are numbered according to those in your main tax return plus any supplementary pages that apply to your circumstances, and although these forms look frighteningly complicated, it is really a question of transferring all the figures into the correct summary boxes and following the instructions to ensure that you do the additions and subtractions according to the right sequence.

If you have capital gains, you will need supplementary sheets (see page 70) and the notes that come with them have additional calculation boxes.

Is there an easier way of checking my tax?
The Tax Calculation Guide that comes with your tax return is difficult to use because it has to cater for every conceivable contingency. In fact, most people will not need to use many of the boxes at all.

If you tax affairs are not too complicated you may find it useful to use the quick tax check reproduced on pages 91–92 – or file your return electronically (see page 89).

How to file your tax return over the internet

If your tax affairs are not too complicated, then you can use the internet to file your tax return electronically. It will depend on the software that you use as to whether you can file all the supplementary forms as well as the basic tax return (SA100). With most commercial versions of tax return software you can file all the supplementary forms electronically; if you just use the Inland Revenue free software package, which you can download from their website, www.inlandrevenue.gov.uk/sa, then apart from the basic tax return (SA100) you can only file the Employment return (SA101), Self Employed return (SA103) and the Land and Property return (SA105). If you need other supplementary forms then you will have to file your tax return manually.

You can only use an Apple Mac computer if you use operating system 10 (or later) and Internet Explorer 4.17 (or later).

You cannot use the internet service if you have already submitted a tax return for the current tax year, or to correct a return.

A word of advice

The basic rule, whether you are filing electronically or manually, is the same – *make sure you have all the information to hand before you start*. If you need any supplementary pages contact the orderline on 0845 9000 404, or download them from www.inlandrevenue.gov.uk otherwise the process will become frustrating and time consuming and vulnerable to error.

You will almost certainly need your P60 and/or P11D form given to you by your employer; your P45 form if you have left an employment during the tax year; statements covering any interest or dividends earned or rents received; a copy of your accounts if you are self employed; and paperwork recording any capital gains tax, etc.

The benefits of filing electronically

- Extended time periods – you have until 30 December instead of 30 September to file your tax return *if* you want any underpayments of tax collected via your tax code – otherwise you have until 31 January.
- The tax calculation is automatic.
- You get an acknowledgement of receipt.
- Repayments are faster than if you filed your tax return manually.
- The service is safe and secure and you can use it 24 hours a day.
- You can view your statement of account (SA300) at any time.

Go to www.inlandrevenue.gov.uk/activate to register – you will need your tax reference number or National Insurance number. Register, and then wait for postal confirmation of your ID and a separate unique activation PIN number. This will take about seven days.

When you have them, enter the user ID and a password (selected by you) and log in. Enter your PIN number and select 'activate'. You must activate within 28 days of receipt of the acknowledgement letter.

Don't forget to destroy the letter advising you of your PIN number for security reasons.

Submission

Proceed to fill in your return and supplementary sheets and check the entries you have made before pressing the submit button on your computer and your tax calculations will be done automatically.

Look over the calculations before submitting so your tax demand (or repayment) doesn't look stupid (for example, you put your bank interest in as £50,000 instead of £5,000!).

Print out a hard copy to check and keep.

What happens next?

Once you have filed your tax return, you will get an e-mail acknowledging receipt. A statement of account will also be accessible and this will be updated during the course of the year. This will also tell you when payments have to be made. Any refunds will be paid to you automatically unless you have requested that they be accounted for by a change in your PAYE code number.

Helpline

The telephone number of your Inland Revenue office should be shown at the top of your tax return; alternatively telephone the self assessment helpline on 0845 9000 444.

A quick tax check

This quick tax check will be useful for the majority of taxpayers, but will not cover every conceivable variation.

The layout is designed for the year ended 5 April 2004 but you could use it for earlier years provided you alter the tax rates and include those allowances that have since ceased.

Do not include any income that is tax free (e.g. PEPs, TESSAs, ISAs, the first £70 interest on National Savings ordinary accounts or National Savings Certificate interest).

	Tax deducted	Gross amount
Your non-savings income		
Salary or wages after deducting any pension scheme contribution or payroll giving	....	....
State pension		....
Other pensions	....	....
Benefits from employer (see P11D form)		....
Profits from self-employment (usually the accounts period ending in the 2003–2004 tax year) or freelance earnings, after capital allowances and loss relief		....
Casual earnings, after expenses	....	....
Social security benefits that are taxable		....
Income from land and property, after expenses (exclude tax-free rental under Rent-a-room scheme)		....
Total non-savings income	(a) £....................	(A) £....................
Less: allowable expenses		
Personal pension contributions, including retirement annuity contributions for this year (exclude any carry-back to previous year and contributions deducted from salary under PAYE above)	....	....
Charitable covenant or gift aid donations	....	....
Interest paid on qualifying loans	....	....
Other expenses allowed for tax	....	....
Total allowable expenses	(b) £....................	(B) £....................
Savings income (excluding dividends)		
Interest received	....	....
Dividend income		
Dividends received (you should add the tax credit to this and then show it separately in the tax deducted column)	....	....
Total savings and dividend income	(c) £....................	(C) £....................
Total income and tax deducted	a–b+c=(d) £....................	(D) £....................
		A–B+C=D

Less: allowances claim

Personal allowance (but deduct any income
   limit reduction if over 65 – see table on page 97) ....
Blind person's allowance ....
   Income on which tax is payable (D minus total allowances) (E) £ ....

Tax payable

See band limits on page 97 and notes below

First £1,960 of income at 10% ....

Non-savings income

£   at 22% ....
£   at 40% ....

Savings income

£   at 20% ....
£   at 40% ....

Dividend income

£   at 10% ....
£   at 32.5% ....

(E) £   Total (F) £

Less: claim for personal allowances available at only 10%
   Married couple's allowance ....
   Maintenance or alimony (max £2,150) ....
                              (G) £ .... at 10% = (H) £ ....
                                       (F–H=I) £ ....

Less: Enterprise Investment Scheme or
   Venture Capital Trust £   at 20% ....
   CIR relief   £   at 5% ....
                                   £ .... =   (J) £ ....

Less: Tax already deducted   (d) £ ....

Tax due (or refundable if this is a minus figure) I – J – d = K   (K) £ ....
Note: You cannot reclaim the 10 per cent tax credit on dividends.

You will need to add to this sum Class 4 National Insurance liability, any capital gains tax liability and any underpayment from a previous year. (Deduct any tax repayment already received or any potential underpayment already in your tax code for a later year).

Allocation of tax rate bands

You are taxed at 10 per cent of your first £1,960 of taxable income, whatever its source.
Then you pay 22 per cent on the next £28,540 of earned or pension income, or 20 per cent of savings income, and 10 per cent on dividend income if you are not a higher-rate taxpayer. After that, you pay 40 per cent on everything except dividend income which is charged at 32.5 per cent.

Reference notes

Keep notes throughout the year of all changes in your circumstances, your income and expenses, investments and savings so you have everything to hand when you come to fill in your tax return.

Employment income and pensions

_____
_____
_____
_____
_____
_____

Other income

_____
_____
_____
_____
_____
_____

Child tax credit and working tax credit from 6 April 2003

(NB: Any claim for child tax credit will be paid directly to the person looking after a child, not through the tax system.)

_____
_____
_____
_____
_____
_____

Expenses notes

_____
_____
_____
_____
_____
_____

Pension credit

_____
_____
_____
_____
_____
_____

Pension scheme information

_____
_____
_____
_____
_____
_____

Company car details and other benefits

_____
_____
_____
_____
_____
_____

Savings accounts

_____
_____
_____
_____

PEP details

_____
_____
_____
_____
_____

TESSA details

_____
_____
_____
_____
_____
_____

TOISA details

_____
_____
_____
_____
_____
_____

ISA details

_____
_____
_____
_____
_____
_____

Investment notes

_____
_____
_____
_____
_____

Dividends, interest, etc.

_____
_____
_____
_____
_____
_____

Payroll giving schemes and gift aid amounts

_____
_____
_____
_____
_____

Deeds of covenant

_____
_____
_____
_____
_____
_____

House and mortgate data

_____
_____
_____
_____
_____
_____

Gifts received/made

_____
_____
_____
_____
_____

Family matters (children's income), etc.

_____
_____
_____
_____
_____
_____

PAYE Code numbers

_____
_____
_____
_____
_____

Insurance matters
(check values every year)

Home and contents ☐

Personal belongings ☐

Life ☐

Accident, etc. ☐

Critical illness ☐

Car(s) ☐

General reminders

_____
_____
_____
_____
_____
_____
_____
_____
_____
_____
_____
_____
_____

> ### *Tax tip* Keeping records
> With self assessment tax legislation, the law requires you to keep all records of earnings, income, benefits, profits, expenses, etc. and all other relevant information for 22 months from the end of the tax year if you are employed, and for 5 years and 10 months if you are self-employed.

Personal reminders

National Insurance number

_____

Tax reference number

_____

Tax office address

_____

_____

_____

_____

_____

Tax returns
2002 Date sent to tax office

_____

_____

_____

2002 Date agreed with Inland Revenue

_____

_____

_____

2003 Date sent to tax office

_____

_____

_____

2003 Date agreed with Inland Revenue

_____

_____

_____

2004 Date sent to tax office

_____

_____

_____

2004 Date agreed with Inland Revenue

_____

_____

_____

Notes on correspondence

Rates of tax and allowances

Income tax

	2004–2005	2003–2004	2002–2003
Starting rate at 10 per cent	£2,020	£1,960	£1,920
Basic rate at 22 per cent	£2,021–£31,400	£1,961–£30,500	£1,921–£29,900
Higher rate at 40 per cent	over £31,400	over £30,500	over £29,900

Savings income: Once the starting rate income band has been used, savings income (excluding dividends) is taxed at 20 per cent (not basic rate) if you are a basic-rate taxpayer; once your income takes you into the higher-rate band then savings are taxed at 40 per cent.

Dividend income is taxed at 10 per cent for income below the basic rate limit and 32.5 per cent above it.

Capital gains tax
The rate for individuals is the same as their income tax rate.

	2004–2005	2003–2004	2002–2003
Exemption limit	£8,200	£7,900	£7,700

Inheritance tax

	2004–2005	2003–2004	2002–2003
Rate 40 per cent. Exemption limit	£263,000	£255,000	£250,000

Personal allowance

	2004–2005	2003–2004	2002–2003
Aged under 65 (basic level)	£4,745	£4,615	£4,615
†Aged 65–74	£6,830	£6,610	£6,100
†Aged 75 and over	£6,950	£6,720	£6,370
Married couple's allowance (see note)			
‡Aged 65–74	★£5,725	★£5,565	★£5,465
‡Aged 75 and over	★£5,795	★£5,635	★£5,535
Minimum amount	£2,210	£2,150	£2,100
Income limit	£18,900	£18,300	£17,900

Blind person's allowance

	2004–2005	2003–2004	2002–2003
Blind person's allowance	£1,560	£1,510	£1,480

Children's tax credit

	2004–2005	2003–2004	2002–2003
Maximum	Replaced by child tax credit	Replaced by child tax credit	§★£5,200

Notes

★Relief is restricted to only 10 per cent.

The married couple's allowance is available only to couples where either the husband or wife was born before 6 April 1935 or where one person born before this date has married on or after 6 April 2000.

†These allowances are reduced by £1 for every £2 that your income (before allowances) exceeds the income limit (shown above) but the allowance cannot fall below the personal allowance basic level.

‡These allowances are reduced by £1 for every £2 that your income exceeds the income limit but they cannot be reduced below the minimum amount. The personal allowance restriction (†) is applied before restricting the married couple's allowance.

§This was doubled to £10,400 for qualifying children born after 5 April 2002.

Useful contact numbers

If you want to order supplementary tax return sheets
telephone: 0845 9000 404
fax: 0845 9000 604

If you want to download the tax forms from the internet
www.inlandrevenue.gov.uk/sa
e-mail: saorderline.ir@gtnet.gov.uk

If you want to file your tax return electronically
www.ir-efile.gov.uk/
or telephone: 0845 605 5999

If you want general tax advice on the self-assessment helpline
telephone: 0845 9000 444

If you are on a low income and have had tax deducted from bank or building society interest, etc. which you could claim back
telephone the taxback helpline: 0845 077 6543

If you want details or help with the child tax credit
telephone: 0845 300 3900 (helpline)

If you want advice on the Pension Credit
telephone: 0800 99 1234 (claim line)
telephone: 0808 800 6565 (Help the Aged helpline)

If you are newly self-employed
telephone: 0845 915 4515 or
0845 766 0830 in the Welsh language

If you want to claim the working tax credit
telephone: 0845 300 3900

Winter fuel allowance queries
telephone: 0845 915 1515

National Savings enquiries
telephone: 0845 366 6667

Useful booklets
The following Inland Revenue booklets are also available from tax offices or from the internet on www.open.gov.uk/inrev/irleaf.htm

IR3	Personal pension schemes (including stakeholder pensions)
IR34	Pay As You Earn
IR65	Giving to charity by individuals
IR90	Tax allowances and reliefs
IR110	A guide for people with savings
IR120	You and the Inland Revenue
IR121	Income tax and pensioners
IR124/125	Using your own car for business
IR136	Income tax and company vans: a guide for employees and employers
IR139	Income from abroad
IR170	Blind person's allowance
IR171	Income tax: a guide for people with children
IR172	Income tax and company cars
FS1(MCA)	Married couple's allowance restriction
WTC1	Child tax credit and working tax credit: An introduction
WTC5	Help with the costs of child care

Significant dates for your diary

Tick the check boxes when you have completed the tasks.

2004 tax return

31 January 2004
Make first payment on account if applicable
(see page 38) ☐

April 2004
You should receive a 2004 tax return ☐

April/May 2004
Request any supplementary pages from tax
office (ring 0845 9000 404 or fax 0845 9000
604) ☐

31 July 2004
Make second payment on account if applicable ☐

30 September 2004
Send in completed tax return ☐

31 January 2005
Send in tax return if you want to calculate your
own tax. Pay any 2003–2004 balance. ☐

Deadline for carrying back pension
contributions ☐

2005 tax return

31 January 2005
Make first payment on account if applicable
(see page 38) ☐

April 2005
You should receive a 2005 tax return ☐

April/May 2005
Request any supplementary pages from tax
office (ring 0845 9000 404 or fax 0845 9000
604) ☐

31 July 2005
Make second payment on account if applicable ☐

30 September 2005
Send in completed tax return ☐

31 January 2006
Send in tax return if you want to calculate your
own tax. Pay any 2004–2005 balance. ☐

Deadline for carrying back pension
contributions ☐

Your tax organiser

When you fill in the self assessment tax return, you only have to put total figures in the various boxes. Use the following work sheets to record your detailed figures.

Use the left-hand columns
Use the columns in the following work sheets to keep a record of how you arrived at these figures, not only as a convenient means of adding them up but also in case the tax office asks for the details.

Use the right-hand columns
Use the columns in the following work sheets to keep an ongoing record throughout this next year as a reminder of significant figures or events during 2004–2005 so that when you get next year's tax return to complete, you have the information at your fingertips.

Income from interest and savings

Paperwork to keep: interest statements, dividend vouchers, National Savings Certificates

What you entered in your 2003–2004 tax return

Reminders to help you fill in your 2004–2005 tax return

Interest received and tax deducted

Interest received and tax deducted

National Savings

National Savings

Tax tip Joint names
Are your investments in joint names? See page 9.

Income from dividends

Paperwork to keep: dividend vouchers, contract notes

What you entered in your 2003–2004 tax return

Reminders to help you fill in your 2004–2005 tax return

Dividends and tax deducted

Dividends and tax deducted

> **Tax tip** Tax credit
> Can you reclaim the tax credit? See page 12.

Other income

Paperwork to keep: receipts and statements for casual earnings and expenses claimed

What you entered in your 2003–2004 tax return

Reminders to help you fill in your 2004–2005 tax return

Other income

Other income

Expenses claimed

Expenses to be claimed

> **Tax tip** Expenses
> Remember to claim expenses. See page 42.

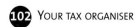

Income from UK pensions, retirement annuities and social security benefits

Paperwork to keep: State pension book or details, P60 form for other pensions, DWP statements

What you entered in your 2003–2004 tax return

Reminders to help you fill in your 2004–2005 tax return

State pension details

State pension details

Other pensions and annuities and tax deducted

Other pensions and annuities and tax deducted

Social security benefits

Social security benefits

Payments allowed for tax

Paperwork to keep: pension statements, interest certificates, covenants, Gift Aid receipts and records, receipts for expenses, etc.

What you entered in your 2003–2004 tax return

Reminders to help you fill in your 2004–2005 tax return

Payments to retirement annuity contracts

Payments to retirement annuity contracts

Payments to personal pension plans

Payments to personal pension plans

Additional voluntary contributions

Additional voluntary contributions

> **Tax tip** AVCs
> Top up your pension contributions before the tax year ends. See page 18.

Maximum contributions allowable for tax as a percentage of your earnings

Age at beginning of tax year	Retirement annuity premium %	Personal pension plan %	Age at beginning of tax year	Retirement annuity premium %	Personal pension plan %
up to 35	17.5	17.5	51 to 55	20.0	30.0
36 to 45	17.5	20.0	56 to 60	22.5	35.0
46 to 50	17.5	25.0	61 to 74	27.5	40.0

What you entered in your 2003–2004 tax return

Reminders to help you fill in your 2004–2005 tax return

Expenses claimed (subscriptions, loan interest, maintenance, etc.)

Expenses claimed (subscriptions, loan interest, maintenance, etc.)

Charitable giving (covenants)

Charitable giving (covenants)

Gift aid (cash donations)

Gift aid (cash donations)

Gift aid (securities or property)

Gift aid (securities or property)

Employment

Paperwork to keep: P60, P45 and P11D forms, receipts for benefits, invoices for expenses, etc.

Diary note

P60 due from employer by	31 May 2004
P11D due from employer by	6 July 2004
Check your PAYE code	Feb/Mar 2004

What you entered in your 2003–2004 tax return

Diary note

P60 due from employer by	31 May 2005
P11D due from employer by	6 July 2005
Check your PAYE code	Feb/Mar 2005

Reminders to help you fill in your 2004–2005 tax return

Changes in employment (dates, P45 details)

_____
_____
_____
_____

Changes in employment (dates, P45 details)

_____
_____
_____
_____

Car mileage log

_____
_____
_____
_____

Car mileage log

_____
_____
_____
_____

Car changes (list price, CO_2 emissions, etc.)

_____
_____
_____
_____

Car changes (list price, CO_2 emissions, etc.)

_____
_____
_____
_____

Benefits received from employer

_____
_____
_____
_____

Benefits received from employer

_____
_____
_____
_____

Expenses claimed

_____
_____
_____
_____
_____
_____

Expenses to be claimed

_____
_____
_____
_____

Tax tip Expenses
Check what's available. See page 43.

Income from land and propery

Paperwork to keep: record of rents received, records of expenses and bills for them

What you entered in your 2003–2004 tax return

Reminders to help you fill in your 2004–2005 tax return

Rent-a-room scheme

Rent-a-room scheme

_____

_____

_____

_____

Rent income received

Rent income received

_____

_____

_____

_____

Expenses claimed

Expenses to be claimed

_____

_____

_____

_____

Foreign income and expenses

Paperwork to keep: overseas dividend vouchers, details of pensions, foreign tax assessments, etc.

What you entered in your 2003–2004 tax return

Reminders to help you fill in your 2004–2005 tax return

Income and tax paid

Income and tax paid

_____

_____

_____

_____

_____

Expenses claimed

Expenses to be claimed

_____

_____

_____

_____

_____

Self-employment and partnerships

Paperwork to keep: all accounts and records, sales and purchase invoices

Diary check
VAT limit OK? ☐
NI payments OK? ☐
Payment on account made ....
Accounts completed ☐

What you entered in your 2003–2004 tax return

Other notes

_____
_____
_____
_____
_____
_____
_____
_____
_____
_____
_____
_____
_____
_____
_____
_____
_____
_____
_____
_____
_____
_____
_____
_____
_____
_____
_____

Diary check
VAT limit OK? ☐
NI payments OK? ☐
Payment on account scheduled..........................
Accounts preparation ☐

Reminders to help you fill in your 2004–2005 tax return

Other notes

_____
_____
_____
_____
_____
_____
_____
_____
_____
_____
_____
_____
_____
_____
_____
_____
_____
_____
_____
_____

> ***Tax tip*** **Don't be late**
> There will be interest charges if you are late with
> 'on account' payments. See page 5.

Personal allowances

What you entered in your 2003–2004 tax return

Reminders to help you fill in your 2004–2005 tax return

_____

_____

_____

_____

_____

_____

_____

_____

_____

_____

_____

_____

_____

_____

_____

_____

_____

_____

_____

_____

+--+
| ***Tax tip*** **Personal allowances** |
| Do you need to consider transferring unused |
| allowances to your wife or husband? See |
| page 29. |
+--+

Share options

Paperwork to keep: share option certificates, correspondence from trustees, market valuations

What you entered in your 2003–2004 tax return

Reminders to help you fill in your 2004–2005 tax return

Share options granted, exercised, etc.

Share options granted, exercised, etc.

_____

_____

_____

_____

_____

_____

_____

_____

_____

_____

_____

_____

Income from trusts, settlements, estates, etc.

Paperwork to keep: dividend and interest vouchers, form R185E, trust correspondence

What you entered in your 2003–2004 tax return

Reminders to help you fill in your 2004–2005 tax return

Interest

Interest

Dividends

Dividends

Other notes

Other notes

Capital gains

Paperwork to keep: contract notes for sale or purchase of shares, invoices and letters for sale or purchase of other assets, invoices for allowable expenses

What you entered in your 2003–2004 tax return

Reminders to help you fill in your 2004–2005 tax return

Assets purchased

_____
_____
_____
_____
_____
_____

Assets purchased

_____
_____
_____
_____
_____

Assets sold

_____
_____
_____
_____
_____
_____

Assets sold

_____
_____
_____
_____
_____

Expenses claimed

_____
_____
_____
_____
_____

Expenses to be claimed

_____
_____
_____
_____

Indexation/tapering relief note

_____
_____
_____
_____
_____

Indexation/tapering relief note

_____
_____
_____
_____

Losses brought forward or carried forward

_____
_____
_____
_____
_____
_____

Losses brought forward or carried forward

_____
_____
_____
_____
_____

Inheritance tax

Notes for planning purposes – and have you made a Will?

Notes

Notes

Index